DK
Human Body Encyclopedia

LONDON, NEW YORK, MUNICH,
MELBOURNE, and DELHI

Senior editor Penny Smith
Senior art editor Cheryl Telfer

Editors Ben Morgan, Zahavit Shalev
Additional design Jacqueline Gooden,
Tory Gordon-Harris, Claire Patane, Laura Roberts
Illustrator Peter Bull
Digital illustrator Pilar Morales

Consultants Dr. Penny Preston, Dr. Frances Williams

Publishing manager Sue Leonard
Managing art editor Clare Shedden
Jacket design Victoria Harvey
Picture researchers Marie Ortu, Rob Nunn
Production controller Shivani Pandey
DTP designer Almudena Díaz

First American Edition, 2005

Published in the United States by
DK Publishing, Inc.
375 Hudson Street
New York, New York 10014

07 08 09 10 9 8 7 6 5 4 3

A Cataloging-in-Publication record for this book
is available from the Library of Congress.

ISBN 978-0-7566-0997-9

Color reproduction by Colourscan, Singapore

Printed and bound in China by Toppan

Discover more at
www.dk.com

Contents

Human body

Skeleton and bones

Moving muscles

Brain and senses

Test yourself with the questions at the bottom of each page...

Circles show close-up images you might not otherwise be able to see.

Colored discs contain facts about special topics, such as taste.

"Get into it" activity buttons show you how you can try things out for yourself.

About this book
This book has special features that will show you how to get your hands on as much information as possible! Use the "become an expert" buttons to find out more about a subject on other pages.

Your amazing body

The greatest machine you'll ever own is your body. It's more complicated than any computer, it lasts for a lifetime, and it's yours for free.

Become an expert... on the skeleton, pages **12-13** on digestion, pages **82-83**

Body parts

Your body is made up of hundreds of different parts. You probably know the names of the parts you can see, but there are many more hidden deep inside you.

Hair

Forehead

Ears

Eyebrows

Cheeks

Nose   Eyes

Lips

Teeth

Inside your body

Doctors can see inside your body with special cameras. X-ray cameras take pictures of hard body parts like bones. Other cameras, called scanners, can see soft body parts.

Hands

Fingers

Wrists

Two of everything

Body parts often come in pairs. You have two feet, two eyes, two ears, two lungs, and so on. This means you have a handy spare in case one of them gets damaged.

A chest X-ray shows the bones in your chest. The white shape in the middle is the heart.

What do we call the study of the human body?

Water, water

Water is the most important chemical in your body. About two-thirds of your weight is water.

The ingredients

Your body is made of just a few simple chemicals, plus water.

Carbon is the chemical in diamonds and coal. A fifth of you is carbon.

Iron makes your blood red. You have enough to make one small iron nail.

Phosphorus is in the tips of matches, as well as your bones and teeth.

Sodium and **chlorine** make salt. Blood is one-third as salty as sea water.

Potassium is used in some types of soap. It's also in your body fluids.

Nitrogen is important in muscles. It's also the main ingredient in air.

Robot

No substitute

The human body is too complicated for robots to copy. Robots can copy the way we walk, but they can't think or feel like we do.

Chimps have hands like ours.

Compared to chimps, our bodies look almost hairless.

Chimpanzee

Curiosity quiz

Take a look at the first few pages in this book and see if you can find these pictures.

Being human

Although we look different from animals, our bodies are similar on the inside. Our closest animal relatives are chimpanzees.

What makes you you?

All human bodies work the same way, but everyone is different. Nobody looks, sounds, or thinks exactly like you. You're different because of the way your genes and experience shape you as you grow up.

Fair skin

Green eyes

Curly hair

Black hair

Unique
The shape of your face, the color of your hair, and many other things make you unique— different from everyone else.

Freckles

6

How many genes are there in the human body?

In the genes

Genes are instructions that build your body and tell it how to work. Your genes control many of the things that make you unique, like the color of your eyes or how tall you'll be.

There's enough

DNA

Your genes are stored in a chemical called DNA, which looks like a twisted ladder with four different types of rungs. The rungs make up a four-letter alphabet that spells out your genes, like letters in a book.

DNA inside you to stretch to the Sun and back 400 times.

This girl has a gene that allows her to roll up her tongue. The boy doesn't have the gene, so he can't roll his tongue.

get into it

Look in a mirror and see if you can roll your tongue. Don't cheat by squeezing it with your lips. Test your family to see who has the gene.

DNA can split and copy itself.

Learning to ride a bike changes your brain and your body.

Changing body

Genes don't control everything—experience also shapes you. If you exercise a lot, for instance, your body gets stronger.

In the family

Your genes came from your parents. Half come from your mother and half come from your father. If you look like your parents, it's because you share the same genes.

About 30,000.

Building blocks

Every part of your body is made of tiny building blocks called cells, which fit together like bricks in a wall. Cells are so small that hundreds could fit on the point of a pin.

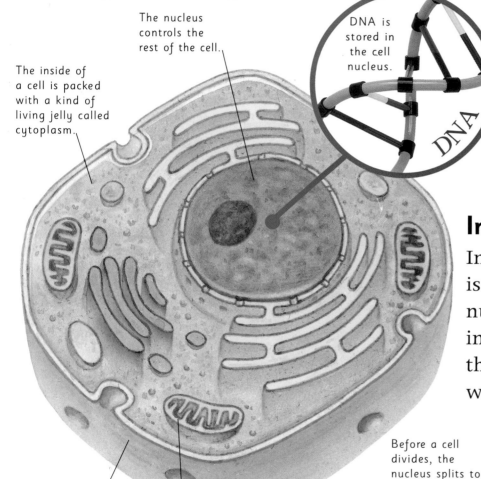

The nucleus controls the rest of the cell.

DNA is stored in the cell nucleus.

The inside of a cell is packed with a kind of living jelly called cytoplasm.

DNA

The skin on your fingertips is made of lots of small ridges.

The outer skin, or membrane, stops things from leaking out.

Tiny generators provide cells with power.

Inside a cell

In the middle of a cell is its control center—the nucleus. The nucleus sends instructions to the rest of the cell, telling the cell what chemicals to make.

Before a cell divides, the nucleus splits to make two nuclei.

Making new cells

A cell makes new cells by dividing. The two new cells are half the size, but they soon grow back. Millions of your cells die every second, but millions of others divide to replace them.

The new cells pull apart and separate, but they usually stay close neighbors.

How many cells are there in the human body?

How big are cells?

Cells are too small to see with the naked eye, but scientists can photograph them through powerful microscopes. The cells on your skin are about a hundredth of a millimeter wide.

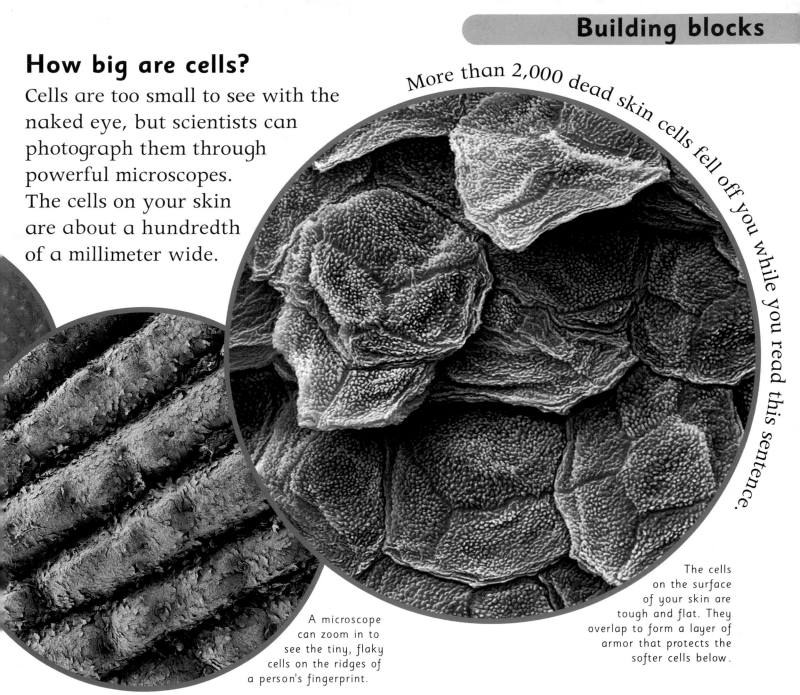

More than 2,000 dead skin cells fell off you while you read this sentence.

A microscope can zoom in to see the tiny, flaky cells on the ridges of a person's fingerprint.

The cells on the surface of your skin are tough and flat. They overlap to form a layer of armor that protects the softer cells below.

Fat cells are bubble-shaped. They store fat under your skin.

Many blood cells are red. They carry oxygen around the body.

Nerve cells are thin and wiry. They carry electrical signals.

Bone cells make your bones hard. They live in tiny holes in bones.

Cells make tissue

Your body contains hundreds of different types of cells that do different jobs. Cells of the same type usually group together to form tissue. Fat, muscle, bone, and nerves are types of tissue. Blood is a liquid tissue.

Organizing the body

Your cells and tissues are organized into larger body parts called organs. In turn, your organs work together to form body systems.

Heart
Kidney
Brain

Organs

An organ is a body part that does a specific job. Your heart's job, for instance, is to pump blood. Kidneys clean blood.

Organ transplant
If a vital organ stops working, doctors may replace it with an organ from another person. This is called a transplant.

Systems
Organs and tissues work in teams to carry out major tasks, like transporting blood or processing food. These teams are called systems.

The heart is the largest organ in the blood system. It pumps blood around the body.

The tubes that carry blood away from the heart are called arteries (shown in red).

The tubes that carry blood back to the heart are called veins (shown in blue).

Heart and blood
Your heart, blood, and blood vessels make up the blood system. It transports vital supplies around your body.

Which body system makes your stomach rumble?

Muscles

Your muscle system is made of tissues that move parts of your body by pulling on them or squeezing them. Your biggest muscles all pull on bones.

Your fingers are moved by muscles in your arm.

Muscles change the position of your skeleton by pulling different bones.

The most powerful muscles are in your legs.

Other systems

Some of your other important systems are shown in this list.

Breathing system: the main organs are your lungs, which take in air.

Hormone system: this uses powerful chemicals to control your body and mood.

Skin, hair and nails: these form your body's protective covering.

Immune system: this seeks and destroys germs that get into your body.

Urinary system: this cleans blood and gets rid of waste chemicals.

Reproductive system: these are the organs that make babies.

Skeleton

Bones and joints make up the skeletal system, an inner frame that supports the body.

A quarter of your bones are in your feet.

Nerves

Your nervous system carries electrical signals around your body. You need this system to see, hear, think, and react.

Signals shoot along nerves to muscles, telling them when to pull.

Senses, such as touch, rely on nerve cells that send signals to your brain.

Your brain is the nervous system's control center.

Digestive system

Your digestive organs break down food to provide your body with energy and raw materials.

Your mouth is the first part of the digestive system.

A long, twisting tube makes up your intestines, where digested food is absorbed.

The digestive system.

Smallest bone

Around the same length as a grain of rice, this is one of the smallest bones in your body. It lies deep inside your ear.

Skull

Jawbone

Neck bones

Did you know that you have seven bones in your neck, the same number as a giraffe? The top one allows you to move your head up and down; the second lets you rotate it from side to side.

Rib

Pelvis

There are 24 bones in your spine.

Skeleton

Your bones all connect to make a frame for your body called the skeleton. This protects your insides, and helps you move around.

Shoulder blade

Each finger has three bones, except for your thumb, which has two.

206 bones

There are 206 bones in an adult skeleton. Over half of these are found in the hands and feet—the parts of your body that perform the most complicated movements.

You have eight small bones in each wrist.

12

Frogs have very short spines to withstand the strain of the huge leaps they take.

A fish's spine allows it to bend its body from side to side so it can swim smoothly.

Other skeletons

Most animals have a backbone and are called "vertebrates." Animals with no spine, like spiders and bugs, are called "invertebrates."

Snakes are incredibly flexible thanks to many identical vertebrae forming their long spines.

Your tailbone is at the very bottom of your spine.

Thighbone

Shinbone

Your ankle has three larger bones and four smaller ones.

There are 54 bones in your hands, and 52 in your feet.

The thighbone is the biggest and strongest in the body.

Long-lasting
Bone is a very hard material and one of the last parts to rot away when a body is buried. This woman lived in the Stone Age, 5,000 years ago, but her bones have survived until today.

Become an expert...
on bone and cartilage, pages 20-21
on teeth, pages 84-85

24, unless you are one of the rare people born with 26.

Head case

The most complex part of the skeleton is the skull. It is made of many bones that fit together tightly, to protect the brain and support the face.

The frontal bone forms your forehead.

The cranium is the domed part of your skull.

Helmet
The upper part of the skull is like a helmet that protects the brain. The lower part forms a structure for your facial features to attach to.

Eye sockets are made up of seven different bones.

The front of the nose has no bones.

The brain fills most of the cranium.

Facial features
This image shows the relationship between your skull and face. There are no bones shaping the front part of your nose, your lips, or your ears. Your nose and ears are shaped by cartilage.

Teeth are set into the upper and lower jaws.

Why does a baby have spaces between its cranial bones?

Back of the head

The spinal cord goes through a large hole in the skull.

Blood vessels pass through small holes in the skull.

Upper jaw

The lower jaw is not shown here.

There are two parts to the upper jaw.

The lower jaw is hinged. It is the only skull bone that can move.

Jigsaw

The skull bones fit together like pieces of a jigsaw puzzle. All but one of the bones are locked in place. This makes the skull very strong.

Hole in the head

From underneath, you can clearly see the big hole at the bottom of this skull. The spinal cord—which runs down your back—meets your brain here.

Face from the past

Scientists can work out what a dead person's face looked like from their skull alone. They examine the facial bones and build up artificial cartilage, muscle, and skin over them.

Meet the relatives

Chimpanzees and humans share a common ancestor. However, chimps have smaller brains than humans, so their craniums are smaller. Chimps also have a large ridge above their eyes, and a jutting jaw.

So its head could withstand being squashed while it was being born.

Bendable backbone

Your spine is a line of bones running down the back of your body. Without it, you couldn't hold up your head and body, or make any kind of movement.

Your spine curves gently, a bit like the letter "S."

The first seven bones are in your neck. They are known as the cervical vertebrae.

The next 12 are called the thoracic vertebrae.

Stack of bones

Your spine contains 24 separate bones called vertebrae. At the bottom are nine more vertebrae. They are much smaller and are fused together.

The thoracic vertebrae form joints with the ribs.

A straight back is actually quite curvy.

The five lumbar vertebrae bear most of your weight.

The fused bones of the sacrum and coccyx don't allow much movement.

Back of spine

Front of spine

The five sacral vertebrae are fused together.

The spinal cord goes through this hole.

The coccyx consists of four fused vertebrae.

Segments of the spine

Each vertebra has a strong, stubby section that supports the weight of your body, and a hole for the spinal cord to pass through.

16

What is a slipped disk?

Shock absorbers

You twist and bend your spine almost every time you move. Sandwiched between the vertebrae are pads of cartilage to stop them from banging and rubbing against each other and getting worn out.

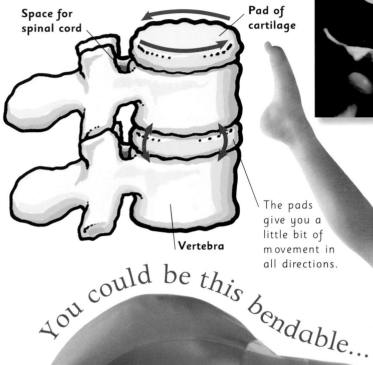

Space for spinal cord

Pad of cartilage

The pads give you a little bit of movement in all directions.

Vertebra

Rib cage

Your thoracic vertebrae connect to your ribs. Together, they form a cage around your heart and lungs. Rib bones are curved. They are also thinner and more bendable than the bones in your spine.

A woman's pelvis is shaped differently from a man's. A baby can pass through it when she gives birth.

Pelvis

Reproductive organs and some digestive organs rest in the bowl-shaped hollow of your pelvis. The sacral vertebrae and coccyx form the bottom of the bowl.

You could be this bendable...

The way the back curves means we can't bend as far back as we can forward.

Bending backbone

The amount of movement between each vertebra and its neighbors is actually very small, but added together, they allow for a large range of movement.

...with a lot of practice!

get into it
Bend over. Gently feel the bones of your spine with your fingertips. Can you follow them from neck to waist?

It's when one of the pads between the vertebrae gets damaged.

Living bone

Their outer surface may be hard and dry but that doesn't mean your bones aren't alive. Bones are always growing and repairing themselves.

What's inside our bones?

Bone accounts for one sixth of your body's weight. Its clever structure means it's often lighter than it looks.

Marrow can be found in the spine, skull, and the main leg and arm bones.

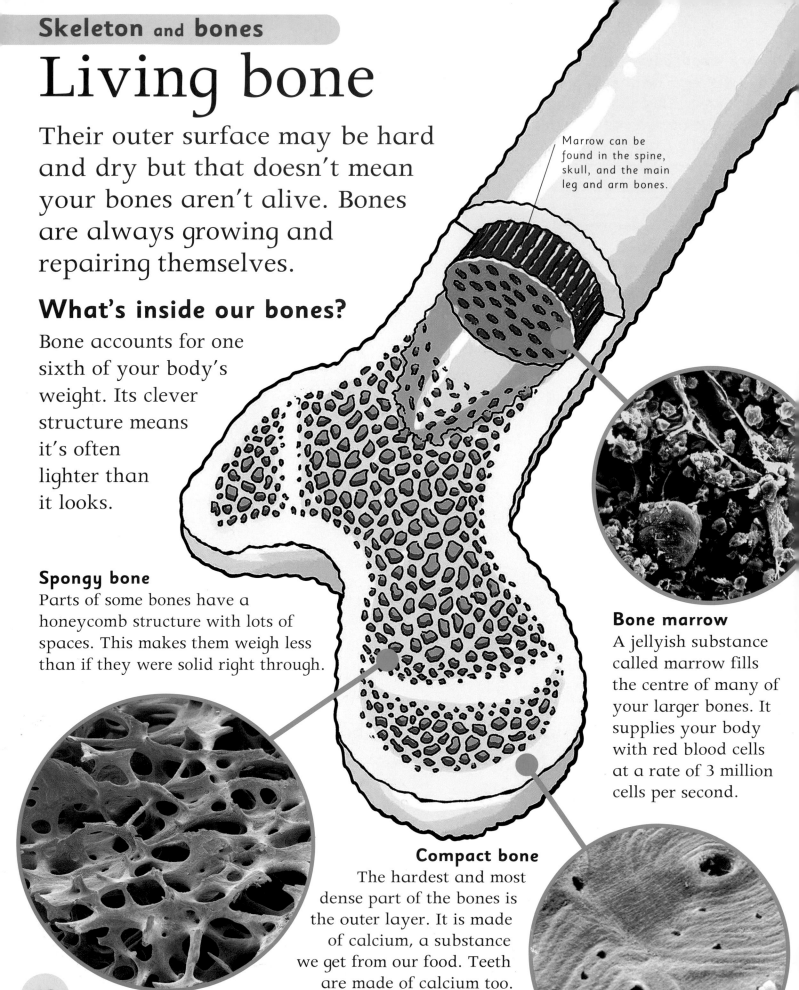

Spongy bone
Parts of some bones have a honeycomb structure with lots of spaces. This makes them weigh less than if they were solid right through.

Bone marrow
A jellyish substance called marrow fills the centre of many of your larger bones. It supplies your body with red blood cells at a rate of 3 million cells per second.

Compact bone
The hardest and most dense part of the bones is the outer layer. It is made of calcium, a substance we get from our food. Teeth are made of calcium too.

What are the most commonly broken bones?

Broken bone

Bones are strong and flexible enough to cope with a lot of pressure, but, as this X-ray shows, they sometimes break. Luckily they can heal themselves.

If the broken bone ends have slipped apart they must be repositioned by a doctor before healing begins.

On the mend

New cells form at each end of the broken bone, closing the gap between them. It takes about 6 weeks for this to happen.

Curiosity quiz

Take a look through the Skeleton and bone pages and see if you can identify where these bony bits come from.

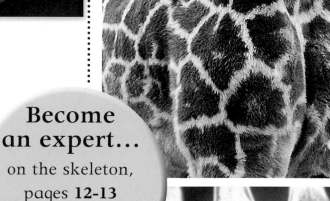

Become an expert... on the skeleton, pages **12-13** on skin and nails, pages **70-71**

Your bones are still growing until your late teens.

Padded clothes help protect bones from sudden impact.

Looking after your bones

Calcium from milk and cheese is needed to build strong bones. Weight-bearing exercise like walking, climbing, or skating helps to strengthen bones.

Fingers, wrists, and arms.

Bone and cartilage

When you were a baby, you were tiny. Slowly, as you get older and bigger, your bones do a clever trick. Not only do they grow, but they also change.

Baby's hand

Making bones

Babies' bones are made out of a soft, flexible material called cartilage. Slowly, this hardens and turns into bone.

Baby bones are entirely made of soft, growing cartilage.

Adolescent bones are mostly bone, with a small amount of cartilage.

Adult bones have stopped growing. Most no longer contain cartilage.

Stick out your ears!

Your ears are made of cartilage, not bone. They are strong, but much more bendable than your bony bits.

More, less

You've got more bones than your mom or dad!
You were born with over 300 "soft" bones, but as you get older, many fuse together. By the time you're 25, you'll have 206 fully formed bones.

Cross-section of an ear—the cartilage sits between two layers of skin.

Which foods are rich in calcium, the mineral you need to grow healthy bones?

Child's hand

Adult's hand

Bone shows up as purple in these X-rays. The difference between the amounts of bone can clearly be seen.

Taller, shorter
Between each bone in your spine are small disks of cartilage. During the day these get squashed, and when you rest at night they spread out again. This means you're a little bit taller in the morning than in the evening.

Cartilage coats the ends of these bones.

The pads of cartilage get squashed from standing up and stretch back out while you're lying down.

Smooth-coated joints
The ends of neighboring bones are covered in smooth cartilage. That way, they can glide against each other when you move.

Moving joints

Joints are the places where bones meet. Different kinds of joints allow you to move in different ways.

Hinge joint

Your knee can bend in the middle, but it can't swing from side to side. This joint has a hinge like the one that allows you to open and close a door.

Fixed joints

The bones that make up your skull start to join soon after you are born. Once they have fused, none of them allow movement except the hinged jaw joint.

Knee joint

Have you ever used a joystick? That's a ball and socket joint!

Ball and socket

Your hips are ball-and-socket joints. They allow you to move your legs in all directions and even to turn them.

There are 19 movable joints in your hand—not counting the ones in your wrist!

What is tennis elbow?

Bending bits

Different kinds of joints all over your body keep you moving.

Neck bones feature a pivot joint that allows your head to turn.

Wrists have a joint that allows them to turn but not go all the way around.

Ankles contain different joints for up-and-down and side-to-side movement.

Your hand is a fantastic feat of engineering!

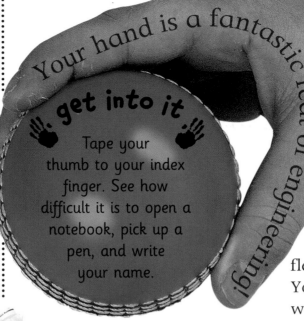

get into it

Tape your thumb to your index finger. See how difficult it is to open a notebook, pick up a pen, and write your name.

Thank your thumbs

Your thumb is the most flexible of your fingers. You rely on your thumbs whenever you handle delicate objects.

Hip hooray

Joints, particularly knee and hip joints, sometimes wear out in old age. When this happens, doctors can remove the worn-out joint and replace it with an artificial one.

This woman has stretchy muscles and ligaments that allow her spine to bend farther than most people can manage.

Ligaments

Bands of tissue called ligaments act like elastic. They hold your bones together yet still allow you to move.

Ligament

Bone

Your elbows have a hinge joint for bending and a pivot joint so they can turn.

Fabulously flexible

People whose joints are particularly flexible are called "double-jointed." The condition can run in families, but people who are double-jointed must practice if they want to keep their ligaments stretchy.

The name for sore elbow tendons caused by overuse.

The body's muscles

Every time you move, you use muscles. Muscles make you walk, blink, and smile. Some muscles work without your thinking about them, but others need to be told to move. They all work by shrinking, which makes them pull or squeeze.

Pulling strings

About 650 of your muscles are wrapped around the bones of your skeleton. They move your body by pulling on the bones. Together, they form the muscle system.

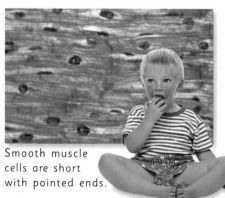

Smooth muscle

This type of muscle makes things move inside your body. It mixes food in your stomach and pushes food through your intestines.

Smooth muscle cells are short with pointed ends.

Heart muscle

When you put your hand on your chest, you can feel your heart beating. Your heart is a strong muscle that squeezes blood around your body.

Heart muscle cells are striped with oval blobs.

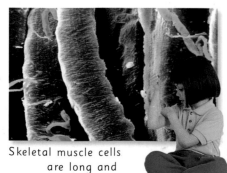

Skeletal muscle

Skeletal muscles pull on bones to change the shape of your skeleton and move your body. These muscles are voluntary, which means you can use thought to control them.

Skeletal muscle cells are long and threadlike.

The pectoralis muscle swings your arm.

The biceps muscle bends your arm.

Your longest muscle is the sartorius. It helps cross your legs.

The tibialis muscle bends your foot.

What weighs more: all your bones or all your muscles?

Muscle magic

Muscles have hundreds of uses. They make up about a third of your body weight.

Largest muscle: you use the muscle in your buttock for sitting and walking.

Fastest muscle: this one makes you blink. It works up to 5 times a second.

Ear wiggling: a few people can control the muscles around their ears.

Smile: a fake smile uses different muscles from a real, involuntary smile.

Who's in charge?

You use hundreds of muscles when you run and jump. Your brain controls them all, a bit like a conductor directing an orchestra. It sends signals along nerves to every muscle, saying exactly when to work and when to rest.

Become an expert ...

on making sounds, pages **64-65**
on how intestines push food, pages **88-89**

Hundreds of muscles work in a carefully controlled sequence when you jump in the air.

Tongue twister

Your tongue is a bundle of lots of muscles that make it super-flexible. It can reach anywhere in your mouth to pull and push pieces of food. Its acrobatic movements are also vital to speech.

Your tongue contains at least 14 different muscles that make it amazingly flexible.

Your muscles.

25

How muscles work

Muscles work by contracting, which means they shorten. As a muscle contracts, it pulls. The larger the muscle, the more powerfully it pulls.

When the biceps muscle contracts, it pulls your forearm and bends your arm.

When the triceps muscle contracts, it straightens your arm.

Working in pairs

Muscles can pull but not push. They work in pairs that pull in opposite directions. When one muscle pulls, its partner relaxes.

Your forearm contains pairs of muscles that move your hand and fingers back and forth.

Fibers in fibers

Skeletal muscles are made of cells called muscle fibers. Inside these are even finer fibers called myofibrils, which contract to make a muscle shorten.

A typical muscle

Bundle of muscle cells

One muscle cell

Myofibrils inside a muscle cell

Where is the body's smallest muscle?

Try raising your ring finger with your hand in this position. It's stuck because it's joined to the same tendon as the middle finger.

Middle finger

Ring finger

Tendons

Muscles are fastened to bones by tough bands called tendons. When you wiggle your fingers, you can see the tendons move on the back of your hand.

A floppy start

A newborn baby has little control over his head or neck muscles. It takes about a month before it can hold up its head, and six months for strong, steady head control.

Getting a stitch

If you run a lot, you may get a pain in your side. This is a stitch. Scientists aren't sure exactly why it happens, but it might be because the muscles and ligaments in your abdomen are working too hard.

Making faces

Muscles in your face are attached to skin as well as bone. They pull the skin when you change your expression. You use about 17 muscles when you smile.

No rest

Muscles work all the time. They hold you upright—without them, you would flop on the floor. Muscles also work when you are asleep, keeping your body firm and toned.

In the ear.

27

Muscle power

The more you use your muscles, the better they get. Active games and exercise make your muscles larger, stronger, and more flexible. They also help you keep going without tiring.

Stamina

If you have stamina, you can keep going for a long time without getting tired. Exercise that makes you feel out of breath, like running, improves your stamina.

Flexibility

When you're flexible, your joints and muscles can move freely and your body can bend and straighten easily. Exercise that stretches your body, such as gymnastics or dancing, improves your flexibility.

This contortionist has made her body more flexible by doing exercises that stretch her back.

Strength

Pushing, pulling, and lifting make your muscles bigger and stronger. Bodybuilders lift heavy weights over and over again until their muscles are enormous.

You need strong muscles to win a tug-of-war.

Become an expert …
on how your heart works, pages **50-51** on healthy food, pages **106-107**

What happens to muscles if you don't exercise?

Body heat

This picture shows the heat of a man's body. Muscles make heat when they work hard, which is why exercise makes you hot. On cold days, your muscles try to warm you up by shivering.

Muscle food

To build strong muscles, you need a type of food called protein. Meat, fish, beans, milk, and eggs are rich in protein.

Most vegetables don't contain much protein.

Milk

Chicken

Fish

Egg

Beans

Fish is a very good source of protein.

Staying in shape

Exercise is very good for your health. As well as making your muscles bigger, it strengthens your heart and lungs.

Walking to school, or going out for walks, builds strength and stamina.

Soccer is great for improving your flexibility and strength.

Swimming strengthens your heart muscle and builds stamina.

Cycling strengthens your leg muscles and builds up stamina.

Dancing keeps your body supple and helps build strength.

They get small and weak.

Headquarters

The brain is the body's control center. It is a complicated organ that works very quickly, a bit like a powerful, living computer.

Sense signals
The cerebrum is the main part of your brain. It gets and stores sense information and also controls your movements.

Cerebrum

Clever calculator
The cerebrum is also responsible for thinking, speaking, and complicated tasks such as addition.

Cerebellum

Your brain stem works at the same rate whether you're awake or asleep.

Brain stem

Muscle control
Your cerebellum helps you to balance and move your muscles. You use this part of your brain when you dance.

24 hours a day
Whatever else you do, the brain stem makes sure your heart and breathing never stop.

Does your brain hurt when you have a headache?

Skull

Brain

In relation to the size of our bodies, humans have the biggest brains of any animal.

Brain box

Your skull is a bony shell that fits together like a jigsaw puzzle around your brain. Shock-absorbing liquid fills the space between brain and skull.

Learning

When you learn to do something, you create connections between cells in your brain. Next time you do it, the connections are already there, so it is easier.

Short-term memory

Your short-term memory only holds information for about a minute. You use it to compare prices when you go shopping, or to remember a name when you meet someone new.

Long-term memory

Your name, phone numbers you know by heart, and skills such as riding a bike can be kept for many years in your long-term memory.

Curiosity quiz

Take a look through the brain and senses pages and see if you can spot where these come from.

No—your brain can't feel pain, but the muscles around your head can.

A good night's sleep

Your body and brain slow down when you sleep, but they don't stop working. Your brain needs sleep to sort out the events of the previous day.

Your knee jumps forward even though your brain hasn't told it to move.

Cross your legs and tap just below the knee.

No need to think

You do some things without needing to think about them. These are called reflex actions and include blinking, coughing, and the knee-jerk reflex.

Network of nerves

All of the body contains nerve cells. These connect to form the network of nerves we call the nervous system. It transports messages between the body and the brain.

Brain

Spinal cord— the center of the network

Nerve cells viewed through a microscope.

Quick as a flash

Nerve cells lie next to one another, forming long chains. They pass messages to their neighbors—a little like a speedy relay race—to and from the brain.

Which is the longest nerve in your body?

Touchy feely

Your skin is in immediate contact with the world. Using your sense of touch allows you to tell if something is hot or cold, dull or sharp, rough or smooth, or wet or dry.

Merkel's disk responds to light touch and is sensitive to the texture of things.

Things we can feel

Skin is packed with many sense receptors. Each sort responds to different sensations.

 Warmth is detected by nerve endings quite close to the surface of the skin.

 Cold is felt by different sensors to heat. Extreme cold registers as pain.

 Deep touch sensors enable you to grip things tightly.

 Light touch sensors lie at the root of hairs on your arms and legs.

 Vibrations from an electric drill trigger vibration sensors.

 Tickly feelings result from a light and unexpected touch.

 Sensitive fingertips full of receptors are able to tell coins apart.

Not worth noticing

Although your brain receives messages all the time, it filters out the less important ones. That's why you're not constantly aware of the clothes against your skin.

Meissner's corpusle senses light touch.

It feels slimy!....

Ouch!

The body has its own system of alarm bells. Pain receptors warn us when a part of the body has been hurt or is about to be harmed.

This girl quickly moves her finger away from the thorn to stop the pain.

How many touch receptors are in a fingertip

Free nerve endings respond to heat, cold, and pain.

The Ruffini ending responds to firm or continuous touch.

Surface of skin

Dermis

Fat

The Pacinian corpuscle responds to firm pressure and vibration.

Under the skin

Dead cells form the surface of your skin. Below that lie sweat glands, hair follicles, and different types of sensory receptors.

.... the message shoots off to the brain....

Sensitive bits

Skin contains more touch receptors than any other part of the body. But some areas are more sensitive than others.

 Fingertips are packed with sensors, especially light pressure receptors.

 Lips have very thin skin which is good at detecting heat and cold.

 Toes are very sensitive, but thick skin makes the heel less sensitive.

Reading by touch

Braille is a system that uses raised dots to represent letters and numbers. It was invented so that people with bad eyesight would be able to read by feeling the page with their fingertips instead of looking at words.

Braille was invented over 150 yeas ago.

B I R D

 get into it

Put one finger in cold water, one in hot, then put both in warm water. The water feels cold to the hot-water finger and hot to the cold-water finger.

About 3,000. That's roughly the same as on the whole of the trunk of your body.

Taste and smell

We need to eat and drink to survive, but taste and smell are what make these everyday activities so enjoyable.

Taste detector

Your tongue is a big muscle covered in clusters of taste buds. Each cluster recognizes a particular kind of taste.

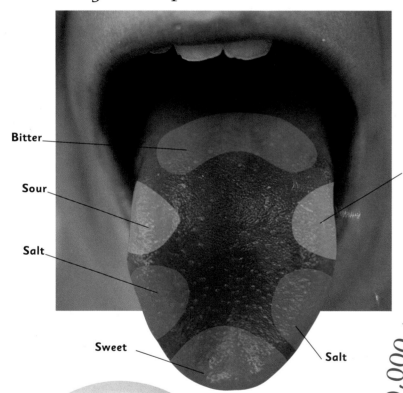

Bitter

Sour

Salt

Sweet

Sour

Salt

Different tastes

There are five types of tastes: bitter, sour, salty, sweet, and umami.

Bitter foods, such as coffee, can be bad for you. Most poisons are bitter.

Sour foods include lemon and vinegar. Food that has "gone bad" tastes sour.

Salt-detecting taste buds can be found on the lips as well as on the tongue.

Sweet foods naturally attract us. Our first food—milk—is sweet.

Umami is the savory taste of foods like soy sauce and mushrooms.

10,000 taste buds are crammed onto your tongue.

get into it
Try putting sugar on different places on your tongue. It tastes sweeter in some places than others. Now try salt, lemon juice, and coffee.

Taste buds
Saliva in your mouth dissolves your food. The food washes over tiny taste buds between the bumps on your tongue. Taste buds recognize different flavors.

How much saliva does an average person produce in a day?

Runny nose

When you have a cold, tiny hairs in your nose get clogged with mucus. This stops them from wafting smell particles deep into your nose and makes it hard to smell or taste things.

Your nose and mouth are linked at the throat.

Sensitive nose

Much of what we think of as taste is actually smell. The back of your nose is linked to your mouth so you can smell your food as you chew it.

Some noses can recognize 10,000 different smells.

Smell receptors

Special cells deep inside your nose recognize scent particles floating in the air. These cells link directly to your brain.

37

Look out!

Sight is the body's main sense and the main way we learn about our surroundings. Two-thirds of the information we take in comes from our eyes.

Wandering eye

Six muscles control each eye. You use both eyes when you look at something, so your eyes move together.

Sclera (or white of the eye)

Iris

Pupil

The middle of the eyeball is filled with fluid.

The muscles surrounding your eyeball make precise movements so you can smoothly track moving objects.

At night, our eyes could detect a lighted candle 1 mile (1.6 km) away.

Pupil

Eyelid

Iris

Sclera

Hidden away

Most of your eye nestles safely in its socket and is protected by pads of fat. On the outside, you can see the iris, pupil, and some of the sclera.

What is the sleep that collects in our eyes?

Tears are made behind each eyelid.

Tears drain into tear ducts. These link to your nose, which is why your nose runs when you cry.

Crying

Tear glands behind your eyes produce drops of salty fluid. When you blink, your eyelids sweep this fluid over your eyes to keep them clean. If something gets into your eye, or you feel strong emotions, the drops turn into floods of tears.

Safekeeping

Your eyes are fragile, squashy balls made of watery jelly, so they need to be well protected.

Bone in your skull surrounds your brain and the backs of the eyes.

Eyebrows sit above your eyes and prevent sweat from dripping into them.

Eyelids and lashes stop dust from entering the eyes and then sweep it away.

Eye color

The iris is the colored part of the eye. All eye colors are produced by one substance, melanin. Lots of melanin results in brown eyes, less means a lighter shade.

Your pupils change size automatically.

Either it's dark or this person has seen something they like.

Pupil size

The pupil is the opening that controls how much light enters your eye. It's smaller in bright light to protect the nerve cells in your eye, and bigger in dim light to let more light in. It also gets bigger when you see something or someone you like.

An iris is as unique as a fingerprint.

Dust and mucus washed from our eyes as we sleep.

How we see

Inside your eye is a lens like the lens of a camera. Its job is to focus light on the back of your eye so you can see things clearly.

Light reflects off an object and enters your eye.

The eye is filled with a semisolid jelly.

Optic nerve

The retina contains cells that sense light.

The lens is clear and flexible. It focuses on things by changing shape.

The pupil is a hole that lets light into the eye.

An object

How your eye works

Light from an object enters your eye through the pupil. It passes through your lens, and makes an upside-down image on the retina at the back of your eye. Cells in your eye send messages down the optic nerve to your brain. Your brain flips the image back the right way round.

Seeing in color

Your eyes contain millions of cells. Cone cells give you color vision but don't work well in dim light. Rod cells work well in dim light but see everything in shades of gray.

What do you call an eye specialist who tests eyesight?

Blurry vision

Sometimes an eyeball is the wrong shape. The lens cannot focus light on the retina, so everything is blurry. Glasses make the light focus in the right place to make things clear.

Short eyeball

If you have a short eyeball, you will have difficulty seeing things close up. This is called farsightedness.

Long eyeball

It is difficult to see objects that are far away when your eyeball is too long. This is known as nearsightedness.

Can you see a number? If not, you may be color-blind.

Color-blindness

Some people cannot tell certain colors apart, especially red and green. This is called color-blindness. It is more common in men than women.

Glasses bend the light entering your eye so it focuses on the retina.

get into it

Close one eye and hold a finger in front of your nose. Open that eye and close the other one. The finger appears to move! Each eye sees things differently.

Contact lenses

These work like mini glasses and sit directly in front of the eye. They're a bit awkward, but once they're in, you can't feel them at all.

Contact lenses are made of very thin plastic.

An optician.

41

Eye to brain

Your brain works out what you're seeing by comparing the images it gets from your eyes to things you have seen in the past. Sometimes it can be fooled!

Your brain combines images from both eyes.

The yellow areas are the parts of your brain that deal with information from your eyes.

Optic nerve

Eyeball

Your blind spot is the part of the eye that can't see anything. It is where the optic nerve leaves the back of your eye.

What can you see?

The dark blue in these pictures shows how much animals can see clearly. Light blue shows what they can see less well.

Humans have to move their heads to see clearly to the sides or look back.

Tigers see well to the front to help them find and catch their prey.

Zebras keep a lookout for movements to the sides so they can avoid attack.

Ducks can see all the way behind them, even while facing forward.

Chameleons see small areas clearly. They swivel their eyes to see all around.

To the brain

Our eyes swivel around constantly, taking in sights and adjusting to focus on different things. The information they collect travels to the brain through the optic nerve at the back of the eyes.

What is it called when you look at something and think it's something else?

Tallest tower

Does the green tower look taller than the others? That's because it's farther along the track and we expect objects farther away from us to look smaller. The colors of the towers also affect the size they seem to be. In fact, all the towers are exactly the same size.

Recognizing objects

Your brain is very clever—it can recognize this car from different points of view. A computer would have to be taught that both these pictures are of the same object.

Certain patterns trick your eyes into seeing movement where there is none.

Do you believe your eyes?

Your brain helps your eyes understand what they see. Sometimes you see things that aren't actually there...

You see a heart even though the edge of the shape isn't there because your brain uses the information it has to fill in the gaps.

An optical illusion.

Listen up

When you shout, you send out invisible sound waves through the air. Your ears pick up the waves and transmit the sound to your brain.

The speed of sound

We don't notice the slight delay between someone's lips moving and the sound actually reaching our ears. It's too fast!

How well can you hear?

Your hearing range is from the highest to the lowest notes that you can hear.

Adults have quite a small range compared to other animals.

Children hear higher notes than adults. Your range shrinks with age.

Cats, dogs, and rabbits can hear much higher notes than people.

Bats have excellent hearing. Their range is five times as large as ours.

Sound travels through the

Headphones feed different sounds into each ear so you feel as if you're surrounded by instruments.

Why two ears?

Sounds normally reach one ear first and then the other. This helps our brains figure out where sounds are coming from and how far away they are.

Why do we have ear wax?

Outer ear

What we call the ear is really just the part that we can see. Sounds are collected here, and funneled inward.

A little help

Partially deaf people may use hearing aids. These make the sounds entering the ear louder and easier to hear.

Middle ear

Sounds arriving here from the outer ear cause the eardrum to vibrate and set off movements in three tiny little bones.

Outer ear

air to your ear.

Ear canal

Bones

Cochlea

Middle ear

Inner ear

Ear drum

Tiny hairs are moved by sounds.

Signals travel along these nerves to the brain.

Inner ear

The moving bones cause vibrations in the liquid deep inside the ear. Tiny hairs in your inner ear pick up these vibrations in the liquid around them. The hairs are attached to nerves that connect to your brain.

To protect the skin lining the ear canal, trap dust, and repel insects.

Balancing act

As well as hearing, ears help you balance. Sensors in your ears work with those in your eyes, muscles, joints, and feet to let your brain know your body's position.

The three semicircular canals deal with balance.

Ear hole

Keeping track

Deep inside your ear are three tiny tubes filled with fluid. They detect the movements your body is making and let your brain know about them.

One tube is for forward and backward movements, another for up and down, and the third for side-to-side movements.

A jellylike knob floats in each tube. Inside it are sensitive hairs that detect movement.

The movements travel along the hairs, through a nerve, to the brain.

Watch your step!

Keeping your balance while walking along a narrow wall takes a lot of concentration. You are responding to information coming from your eyes, muscles, and ears at the same time.

Can astronauts learn to balance in space?

The more you practice, the better you'll be at balancing.

Motion-sickness

Traveling in a car, boat, or plane can make you feel sick. Your eyes tell your brain that you're staying still in the vehicle, but your body says it can feel movement. This confusion is what causes motion-sickness.

Basically, your brain is the boss.

Muscle messages

When you move, sensors in your muscles send messages to your brain. If a movement isn't going right, your brain will make you do things differently.

The brain

get into it

First, make sure there is nothing unsafe nearby for you to crash into. Then spin around and around and make yourself feel dizzy.

Why do you feel dizzy?

The liquid in the tubes of your ear is like water in a cup. When you spin, it continues to slosh around for a while even after you stop. Your brain gets confused about which way around you are, and you feel dizzy as a result.

Yes, but it can take a couple of days to learn how.

Blood flow

Blood is the body's transportation system. Pumped by the heart, it travels around the body in tubes called blood vessels, delivering vital supplies to keep your cells alive.

Tube transport

Blood leaves the heart in large blood vessels called arteries, and it returns in vessels called veins. Between the arteries and veins are tiny vessels called capillaries.

Artery

Vein

Capillary

Around the body

Blood travels around your body, passing through organs on the way. It picks up oxygen in the lungs and food in the liver, then gets rid of waste in the kidneys.

Blood picks up oxygen from the lungs and carries it around the rest of the body.

Each major organ has an artery bringing fresh blood and a vein carrying away used blood.

The aorta is the biggest blood vessel in your body. It is as thick as your thumb. A blue whale's aorta is wide enough to swim through!

The vena cava is your biggest vein.

Lung

Lung

Liver

Stomach

Kidney

Kidney

48

When you cut yourself, what kind of blood vessel does the blood usually come from?

Capillaries

Arteries split into smaller and smaller branches. Eventually they turn into capillaries, which are finer than hairs. Capillaries lead into veins, which come together and get bigger on the way back to the heart.

Capillaries

Arteries

Veins

Artery

Vein

There are about 60,000 miles (100,000 km) of blood vessels in your body.

Become an expert...

on breathing in and out, pages 60-61
on air and oxygen, pages 62-63

From red to blue

The color of blood depends on how much oxygen it contains.

Oxygen-rich blood in arteries is brilliant red.

Oxygen-poor blood in veins is dark purplish-red (shown blue on the diagram).

A capillary.

Boom boom

Your heart is a pump that pushes blood around your whole body. Each time your heart beats, it squirts out a small cupful of blood and refills for the next beat.

Where is it?

Your heart is in the middle of your chest, squeezed between the two lungs. You can feel its beat just left of the bone in the middle of your chest.

Double pump

Your heart is really two pumps in one. One half pumps blood through your lungs, and the other half pumps blood around the rest of your body.

Blood from most of the body enters through the vena cava.

Blood goes out to the body through the aorta.

Blood goes out to the lungs.

One side pumps blood to the lungs...

Blood comes in from the lungs

Vena cava

Aorta

Blood comes from the body.

Blood goes out to the body.

How many times does your heart beat in a year?

One-way system

To keep blood flowing one way only, your heart and most veins contain valves. Your heartbeat is the sound of valves shutting when your heart squeezes.

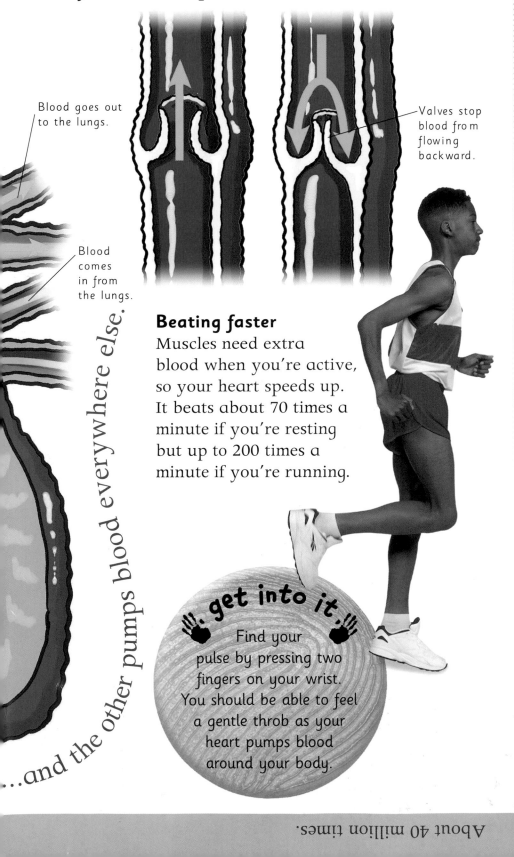

Blood goes out to the lungs.

Blood comes in from the lungs.

Valves stop blood from flowing backward.

...and the other pumps blood everywhere else.

Beating faster
Muscles need extra blood when you're active, so your heart speeds up. It beats about 70 times a minute if you're resting but up to 200 times a minute if you're running.

get into it
Find your pulse by pressing two fingers on your wrist. You should be able to feel a gentle throb as your heart pumps blood around your body.

Curiosity quiz

Take a look through the heart and blood pages and see if you can spot any of the cells and tissues below.

About 40 million times.

All about blood

Blood is a warm, soupy mixture of liquid and cells. The cells carry oxygen and fight germs, and the liquid carries nutrients to body cells and takes away waste.

Main ingredients

Blood contains three types of cells—red blood cells, white blood cells, and platelets. They float in a yellowish liquid called plasma.

One drop of blood contains

5 million red blood cells, half a million platelet cells, 7,000 white blood cells, water, sugar, salt, hormones, vitamins, fat, and protein.

Lots of plasma

Yellow plasma makes up more than half of your blood.

White blood cells seek out and kill germs. They also eat up the dead cells that they meet.

White blood cells and platelets.

Red blood cells make blood red.

Red blood cells transport oxygen from your lungs to the rest of your body.

Become an expert...

on fighting germs, pages **78-79**

on air and oxygen, pages **62-63**

How long does a red blood cell live?

Your blood type

There are four main types of blood, called blood groups. Your blood group affects who you can donate blood to.

People with blood group A can give blood only to people with A or AB.

People with blood group AB can only give blood to others with AB blood.

People with blood group O can donate blood to almost anyone.

People with blood group B can give blood only to people with B or AB.

Blood bank
One in ten people who go to a hospital need extra blood, so hospitals keep a store of blood in a "blood bank." The blood is divided into separate supplies of cells and plasma.

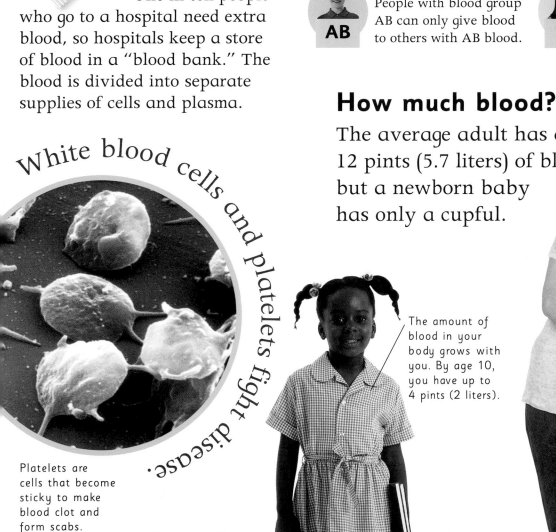

White blood cells and platelets fight disease.

Platelets are cells that become sticky to make blood clot and form scabs.

How much blood?

The average adult has about 12 pints (5.7 liters) of blood, but a newborn baby has only a cupful.

The amount of blood in your body grows with you. By age 10, you have up to 4 pints (2 liters).

By a year old, a baby has more than 1 pint (half a liter) of blood.

About four months.

Blood cells

Nearly half the cells in your body are blood cells. They wear out quickly, so you make three million new ones every second. Most are made in bone marrow, a jellylike tissue in hollow bones.

Red blood cells

The most common cells in your body are red blood cells. They are circular with dimples in each side. Inside, they are packed with a red protein that carries oxygen and is called hemoglobin.

White blood cell

Tiny tunnels

Red blood cells are soft and rubbery so they can squeeze through tiny gaps. In the smallest blood vessels, they travel in single file. All the bumping and squeezing eventually wears them out.

Which cells in the human body contain iron?

Stick together

Platelets are tiny fragments of cells that help blood to clot. They cluster around breaks in blood vessels and grow spiky stalks that help them stick together.

Platelets stick together in a blood clot.

This white blood cell eats pus and germs.

This white blood cell crawls between other cells looking for germs.

Soldier cells

There are lots of different white blood cells, and they all help guard your body against invasion by germs. Some white blood cells creep along the walls of blood vessels and eat any germs they find. Others make chemicals that destroy germs.

Thicker blood

When people climb high mountains, their bodies make extra red blood cells to help them breathe in the thin mountain air. As a result, their blood gets thicker.

Pupils are normally black, but they look red in photographs taken with a flash.

Seeing red

You can often see people's blood in photographs. If you take a picture with a flash, the light reflects off red blood cells in the back of their eyes, turning the pupils red.

Red blood cells.

Bumps and cuts

Blood has the amazing ability to turn from liquid to solid in minutes and help mend cuts in your skin.

Clotting

The moment you cut yourself, your blood starts turning solid, or clotting. The clot quickly plugs the broken blood vessels and stops them from leaking.

Caught in a net

The chemicals released by platelets cause tangled fibers to form in the liquid part of blood. The fibers trap blood cells like fish in a net, forming a solid plug that gets bigger and bigger.

Tangled fibers trap blood cells

Platelets in action

Platelets start the clotting process. They change shape to become stickier and cluster around the cut. At the same time, they release chemicals into the blood.

Platelets in the blood start to work as soon as you get a cut in your skin.

How long does a small cut take to stop bleeding?

Bloodsucker

A leech is a kind of worm that bites your skin and sucks out your blood. Leech saliva contains chemicals that stops blood from clotting. As a result, the cut keeps bleeding until the leech is full.

Leeches live in wet, swampy places. They often slip down people's shoes and bite their feet without being noticed.

First aid

An adhesive bandage can help a cut to heal by closing the skin and keeping out dirt. Bandages also stop you from scratching, which can make a cut worse.

Vampire bats and leeches can stop blood from clotting.

Scabs keep out germs while new skin grows.

Scabs

When a blood clot dries, it forms a scab. New skin slowly grows underneath the scab, repairing the wound. When the skin is ready, the scab becomes loose and drops off.

Bumps and cuts

Painful bumps and cuts are a part of your body's natural healing process.

 A graze is a group of tiny cuts. It forms when something rough scrapes the skin quickly.

 Blisters are bubbles of liquid that form when skin is rubbed a lot. Don't pop them!

 Bruises are patches of blood under the skin. They change color as they heal.

 Black eyes are bruises that form when blood pools under the skin around the eye.

Platelets stick to each other and to other blood cells, causing a clot to start forming.

After a few minutes, the clot is thick enough to stop blood from escaping from the wound.

Between three and eight minutes.

Hormones

A hormone is a chemical that changes the way part of your body works. Even tiny amounts of hormones are powerful. Some work slowly over years, but others have instant effects.

The pea-sized pituitary gland is just under your brain.

Main gland

Hormones are made in parts of the body called glands. The most important is the pituitary gland in your brain. Its hormones control many of the other glands.

Growth hormone

Every day, your pituitary gland releases about eight microscopic doses of growth hormone, mostly when you're asleep. This hormone makes your bones and muscles grow.

The amount of growth hormone you make in one year is less than this tiny pinch of sugar.

Growing up

Toddlers and teenagers have very high levels of growth hormone, which is why they grow so quickly. Adults also make growth hormone, but the level falls with age.

What carries hormones around the body?

Control chemicals

Hormones are very important—they control many body processes.

 Estrogen is the female sex hormone. It turns little girls into adult women.

 Testosterone is the male sex hormone. It turns little boys into adult men.

 Melatonin helps control the daily cycle of sleeping and waking.

 Glucagon raises the level of sugar in your blood, giving you energy.

 Parathyroid hormone tells your bones to release calcium into the blood.

Sugar control

The hormone insulin helps control the level of sugar in your blood. Some people don't make enough insulin and have to check their blood sugar level regularly. They have a disease called diabetes.

People with diabetes prick their skin to get a drop of blood, so they can check how much sugar it contains.

The fright hormone

The hormone adrenaline makes you feel scared or excited. It works in an instant, preparing your whole body for sudden action in case you need to escape from danger.

Adrenaline makes your heart and lungs work harder. Your heart starts to pound and you gasp as your lungs take in extra air.

Your brain becomes alert so you can think quickly.

> **Become an expert ...**
> on growing up,
> pages **102-103**
> on sleep,
> pages **108-109**

Glands above your kidneys release adrenaline.

Your hairs stand on end, making your skin tingle.

Adrenaline travels to your arms and legs and prepares the muscles for action.

Air bags

We have to breathe all the time in order to supply our bodies with oxygen and get rid of carbon dioxide. We use our lungs to do this.

Prepare the air

Before the air reaches your lungs, it travels through your mouth and nose and then goes down your windpipe. It gets warm and damp on its journey.

This flap shuts when you eat so food can't go down your windpipe.

You breathe in through your nose or mouth.

The air travels down your windpipe.

Each lung is a spongy maze of tunnels.

When you breathe in, your lungs stretch out and take in lots of air.

The diaphragm is like a trampoline.

In and out

Your ribs and diaphragm help you to breathe. Your lungs fill with air when you raise your rib cage, then empty out when you lower it. A muscle called the diaphragm helps you do this.

When you breathe out, your lungs squash down, forcing all the air out.

The muscle under your lungs is called the diaphragm. It moves up and down as you breathe.

How many breaths do you take in a day?

A helping hand

Some newborn babies have trouble breathing. They are put into an enclosed cradle called an incubator. Extra oxygen is pumped into the incubator for them.

The view from the bottom of your windpipe.

Windpipe

Air from your mouth and nose enters your windpipe, which goes down your throat into your chest. Then it splits into two passages—one for each lung.

The alveoli are surrounded by tiny blood capillaries to take the oxygen around the body.

Air sacs

Your lungs are full of tunnels ending in tiny air sacs called alveoli. Here, oxygen from the air passes into your blood. Your blood carries oxygen around every part of your body.

Curiosity quiz

Take a look through these images related to breathing. You should be able to find them all in the next few pages.

Air and oxygen

The air you breathe contains a life-giving gas called oxygen. Oxygen helps your cells get their energy from food. They would die within minutes if you stopped breathing.

Oxygen

During the day, trees take in carbon dioxide from the air and give out oxygen.

Oxygen from trees
Trees help to clean the air by filtering out pollution. They also make oxygen, which they release through their leaves.

Carbon dioxide

You normally take about 20 breaths per minute—more if you're exercising.

Become an expert...

on cells, the body's building blocks, page **8-9**

What is in air?
Air is all around you, but you can't see, smell, or taste it. You can feel it when the wind blows.

Out of breath
Breathing heavily gives your body extra oxygen so it can work harder. You feel out of breath and pant when your lungs can't supply your body with oxygen quickly enough.

What is the kiss of life?

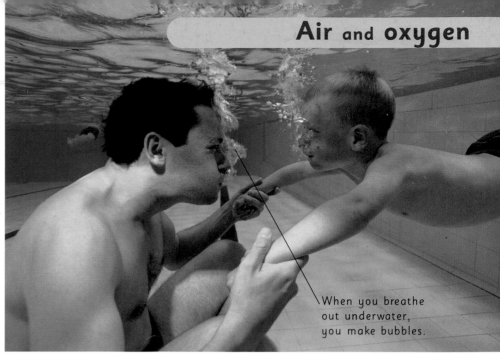

When you breathe out underwater, you make bubbles.

Airless places

Not every place has air to breathe, so sometimes people carry their own.

Fires burn up oxygen and produce thick, poisonous smoke.

Mountaintops have thin air with little oxygen.

Space and the planets near Earth have no air to breathe.

Water contains oxygen, but humans cannot breathe it.

Hold that breath!

People can spend a few moments under water without breathing. Most people can manage about a minute, but the world record is around six minutes.

On a cold day, you can see the water in your breath turn to steam as it meets the air.

You need to be able to control your breathing to blow up a balloon.

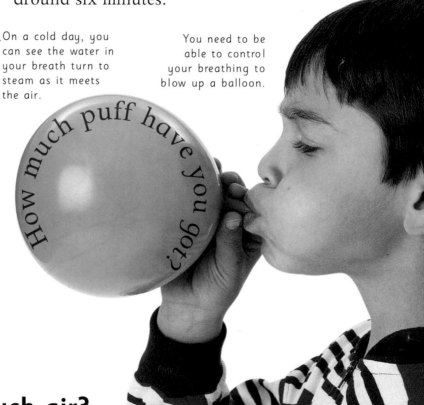

How much puff have you got?

Wet air

Have you noticed that when you breathe onto a window or a mirror, it becomes wet? That's because the air you breathe out is slightly damp.

How much air?

You take in about a pint (half a liter) of air with each breath. If you breathe in deeply, you can take in about 3 quarts (liters) in one gulp.

A way of helping someone who has stopped breathing by blowing into their mouth.

Making sounds

Humans can make many more sounds than other creatures. Because the shape of your face affects your voice, your voice is unique.

You can speak, whisper, hum, and shout!

Voice box

Your voice box has two jobs. You use it to make sounds, and to seal off your windpipe when you eat so you don't choke.

Open vocal cords

Closed vocal cords

Vocal cords

Inside your voice box are two flaps called vocal cords. You make sounds by pushing air between them, causing them to vibrate. Fast vibrations produce high sounds, slower ones, low sounds.

Adam's apple

During puberty, a boy's voice box grows bigger, giving him a deeper voice. You can sometimes see it bulging at the front of the throat. It is known as the Adam's apple.

Adam's apple

Air supply

You use the air coming out of your lungs to produce sounds. So it's difficult to speak when you're breathless.

Why do babies and children have higher voices than adults?

Loud sounds

The harder air is forced out of the lungs, the louder the sound. So when a baby takes a big gulp of air, you can expect a really big cry!

Do you know a snorer?

zzzZZZ

Shaping words

The air coming from the lungs is shaped by the tongue, cheeks, and lips to form specific sounds.

Oo is made by pursing your lips and pushing them out.

Ah sounds are made with a low tongue and a wide open mouth.

Ee is made by stretching your lips and keeping your tongue up high.

zzzzz

Snoring

Sometimes, when people sleep, the fleshy parts at the back of the nose and throat vibrate as they breathe. This rattling is called snoring. It can also happen when you have a cold.

Didgeridoo

Making music

You control your breath when you speak, but you need really excellent breath control to sing or play a wind instrument.

Become an expert...
on puberty, pages **102–103**
on body language, pages **112–113**

They have shorter vocal cords, which vibrate faster, producing higher sounds.

Ah-choo!

You need to keep your airways clear to breathe at all times. If something gets into your airways, you have to get it out pretty quickly!

A sneeze can travel as fast as a car!!!!

Sneezing

Sneezes are a quick way to get rid of unwanted particles that you have accidentally breathed into your nose.

Why do you close your eyes when you sneeze?

The flap
closes when
you swallow.

Usually the flap
is up, holding your
windpipe open.

Gulp!
The sticky mucus (snot) in your nose and airways traps dust and dirt in the air that you breathe. Every day, you swallow about a glass of the stuff.

Safety catch
Unlike other animals, human beings use the throat both for eating and breathing. The epiglottis is a small flap of cartilage that shuts off your windpipe when you swallow so food can't accidentally go down it and choke you.

Nose hairs
The tiny hairs in your nose work like brooms to sweep out any particles that you've breathed in. They get trapped in mucus and are swept along to be swallowed down your throat.

get into it
Yawning is catching! Is there anyone nearby? Give a yawn and see if you can start a yawning epidemic!

Coughing
Irritating particles that have entered your throat are thrown out when you cough. Coughing uses your vocal cords, which is why a noise comes out with the cough.

Hiccups
Sometimes your diaphragm suddenly tightens, causing air to rush into your lungs. This makes your vocal cords snap closed with a "hic." Hiccups seem to happen for no reason.

Yawning
Nobody knows why we yawn, but we do know one effect of yawning: more oxygen in the lungs. It seems we yawn to perk ourselves up when we're feeling tired or bored.

To stop your eyeballs from popping out of your face with the force of the sneeze.

All wrapped up

Skin covers your whole body. It protects you from germs, water, and sunshine, and helps keep your body at the right temperature.

The skin on your eyelids is the thinnest on your body.

Two layers

Your skin has two main layers. The top one—the one you can see—is called the epidermis. Underneath is the dermis, where there are nerves and blood vessels.

There are flat cells on the surface of your skin. These are made from a tough material called keratin. When the cells die, they dry out and flake off.

Skin cells lower down replace the dead ones that flake off.

Skin is a kind of stretchy overcoat.

Waterproof seal

Skin stops water from getting into your body when you swim or take a shower. It also stops fluids from escaping from inside you.

Magnified skin flakes

House dust

Dust is mostly made of dead skin. Dust mites feed on this skin. They live in beds, pillows, and carpets.

Dust mites aren't really this big! They're so small you can't see them.

Heavy load

Skin is the heaviest single part of your body. It can weigh as much as a bag of groceries.

The thickest skin on

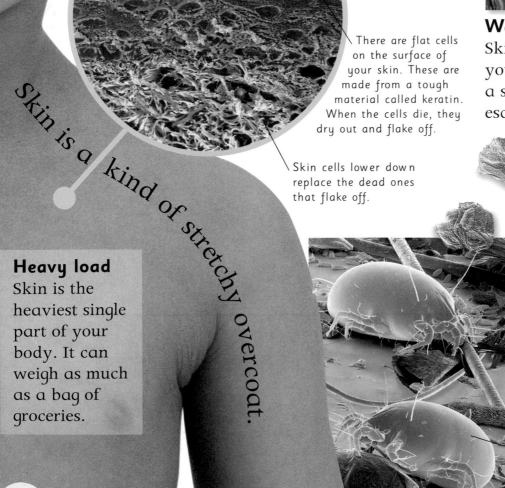

How many dead skin flakes fall off every day?

Sweat

Sweat pore

Sweat gland

If you uncurled a sweat gland, it could be over 3 ft (1 m) long.

Skin color

The color of your skin is affected by a substance called melanin. The more melanin you have, the darker you will be. When you are outside in the sun, your body produces extra melanin to protect your skin. This melanin makes your skin darker and you get a suntan.

your body is on the soles of your feet.

Soggy skin

When you soak in water for a long time, the top layer of your skin gets waterlogged and wrinkly.

Cooling down

When sweat dries on your skin, it helps to cool you down. Sweat comes from coiled tubes under the surface. It gets out through tiny holes called pores.

At your fingertips

Nails work with skin to protect your body. They stop you from hurting the ends of your fingers and help you to pick things up.

Your fingertips have the most sensitive skin on your body.

get into it
Roll the soft part of your fingertip on an ink pad. Now roll your inky fingertip on a piece of paper. The mark you make is your very own fingerprint.

Arch

Loop

Whorl

Fingertip patterns

Fingertips are covered with swirly ridges that help you grip things. These are called fingerprints. Everyone has different fingerprints with different patterns such as arches, loops, or whorls.

The skin around your joints is loose and saggy so you can bend them easily.

On the surface

To the naked eye, your hand looks smooth and solid.

Sweat leaves almost invisible marks on all the surfaces you touch.

Police use fingerprints to help catch criminals.

Under a microscope, you can see all the folds and flakes of dry, dead skin.

Why do you get white spots on your nails?

Nails grow from a root under your cuticle.

— Cuticle

Fat

Bone

When you look at nail keratin close up, it has lots of flaky layers.

The inside story

Although nails are much harder than skin or hair, they're made from the same basic material. It is called keratin.

Our nails are like animals' claws.

Family connections

Like humans, birds and animals have body parts that are made of keratin.

Claws look like nails, but they are stronger and sharper.

Beaks are very hard so birds can tear food and crack seeds.

Holding on

It would be difficult to hold heavy things if you didn't have fingernails. They help to make your fingertips straight and strong. The other reason you have fingernails is so you can scratch when you're itchy!

Nail growth

Nails start to grow before you're born, and they keep going for your whole life. They grow faster on your hands than on your feet.

Horns contain different kinds of keratin. Rhino horns are made of hair keratin.

71

These spots mean the new nail has been bumped or knocked.

Fairly hairy

Hair is mostly made of keratin, just like skin and nails. You have about 100 thousand hairs on your head and millions more on your body.

Hair grows for up to seven years before it falls out.

Hair close up

Each hair is covered with scales that overlap like roof shingles. This makes the hair strong and protects it. Hair is dead tissue, which is why it doesn't hurt to cut it.

What's your hair like?

Hair grows out of tiny pockets or follicles. The shape of these pockets controls whether hair is straight, wavy, or curly.

Like molds, follicles shape each strand of hair. Straight hair grows out of straight follicles.

Slightly curvy follicles produce wavy strands of hair.

Head hair

Lots of body heat escapes from your head, so the hair there is long and thick to keep your brain warm. Fine hairs cover every other part of you except the palms of your hands, the soles of your feet, and your lips.

How many hairs do you lose from your head every day?

Smooth surface

Some men lose their hair as they grow older. In fact, the hair still grows, but it is shorter and falls out more easily. A few people are born without any hair at all—not even eyelashes.

Color chart

Hair, like skin, gets its color from a chemical called melanin. If you have no melanin in your hair, it will be white— if you have lots, it will be jet black.

Brrrr...

When you're cold, tiny muscles pull your body hair upright so it forms a fuzzy layer to keep warmth in. When the muscles pull, they make little ridges called goose bumps.

Goose bump

Follicles that are very swirly in shape produce tightly curled hair.

Good food

If your head is itchy, you may have head lice. These creatures cling to your hair and suck blood from your scalp. When you play with friends, the lice crawl from one head to another. These picky bugs like clean heads best.

Germs

Your body is a walking zoo. It's covered with bugs that feed and breed on you but are mostly too small to see. Many do no harm, but some, called germs, make you sick when they get inside you.

Viruses spread through the air in coughs and sneezes.

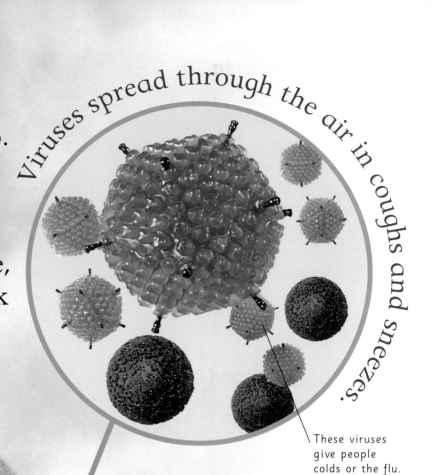

These viruses give people colds or the flu.

Vile viruses

Viruses are the smallest living things on Earth. They break into cells and force them to make new viruses. Viruses can cause colds, flu, measles, mumps, and warts.

Become an expert...

on clearing airways, pages **66-67**
visiting the doctor, pages **110-111**

Wart
A wart is a patch of thickened skin caused by a virus. The virus often spreads from person to person in places where people walk barefoot, such as swimming pools.

What animal has killed more people than any other?

Beastly bacteria

Bacteria are very common germs that often spread by touch. When bacteria get into cuts, they cause swellings and sores. Certain types cause deadly diseases if they get into your stomach or lungs.

Your hand leaves bacteria on anything you touch

Billions of bacteria

There are more bacteria on your skin than there are people in the world. Most do little harm, and some actually protect you from other germs. If you touch rotten food or feces, your hands will pick up more dangerous bacteria.

Big bugs

Creatures much bigger than bacteria or viruses also feed on your body and can make you sick.

Giardia live in intestines and spread in dirty water. They cause diarrhea.

Threadworms live in the large intestine and spread on dirty fingers.

Follicle mites live in the roots of most people's eyelashes and do little harm.

Mosquitoes suck people's blood and can spread germs that cause deadly diseases.

Fungi

Some germs are fungi (related to mushrooms). Tinea (ringworm) is a type of fungus that grows through skin like a plant, sending out long thin shoots.

The tinea fungus grows through your skin like a plant, sending out long thin shoots.

Body defenses

Although you can't see them, germs are always landing on your body and trying to get inside it. Your body has lots of clever ways of keeping them out.

Poison tears
Germs that land on your eyes are washed away by tears, which come from glands above your eyes. Tears contain the chemical lysozyme, which kills bacteria by making them burst open.

You make about a quart (liter) of saliva a day.

Saved by spit
The liquid in your mouth is called saliva. As well as helping you digest food, saliva protects your mouth, tongue, and teeth from attack by bacteria.

Ear wax flows slowly out of your ears all the time, flushing out dirt and germs.

Sticky business
Germs get into your lungs when you breathe in. They get trapped in a sticky liquid called mucus, which lines your airways. Tiny beating hairs continually push the mucus up to your throat to be swallowed.

76

Which is your largest defensive organ?

Acid attack

Glands inside of your stomach make acid, which kills germs you've swallowed. Your digestive system then breaks down the germs along with your food.

Yuck!

The feeling of disgust protects you from germs. Anything that smells revolting or looks horrible is probably full of germs. Disgust stops you from touching it.

Become an expert...

on eyes, pages **38–39** on digesting food, pages **88–89**

Slimy guts

The inside of your intestines are covered with slimy mucus, which stops germs from getting into your blood. Your large intestine also contains millions of "friendly" bacteria, which prevent other germs from growing.

Your skin.

Fighting germs

If germs break through your outer defenses and invade your tissues, your body fights back. The cells of your immune system hunt and destroy germs. This system also remembers germs and protects you from them in the future.

Antibodies attacking germs.

Killer cells

White blood cells called macrophages kill germs by swallowing them. When a macrophage finds a germ, it stretches out, wraps around the germ, and pulls it inside. Digestive juices then destroy it.

Antibodies

Some white blood cells make chemicals called antibodies. These stick to the surface of germs, telling other body cells to attack.

Antibody

This germ is being swallowed.

This white blood cell is called a macrophage.

Heating up
Your body gets hotter when it fights germs, which gives you a fever.

How many tonsils are in your throat?

Extra protection

Doctors protect you from germs with vaccines. Vaccines contain weak or dead germs that your immune system learns to attack. If the real germ ever gets inside you, your immune system remembers it and attacks very quickly.

Killer milk

Breast milk contains germ-killing antibodies that protect babies from disease. During the first few days of a baby's life, the mother makes a special milk called colostrum, which is packed with antibodies.

Lymph system

Fluid continually leaks out of your blood vessels and tissues. It returns to the blood through tubes called lymph vessels. Dotted along these are swellings called nodes, which filter out germs.

The swellings in lymph vessels are called lymph nodes.

Tonsils

At the back of your mouth are several patches of tissue called tonsils. They are full of white blood cells that fight germs in your throat. However, the tonsils sometimes fill with germs themselves and have to be removed.

79

Two main ones and four smaller ones.

Allergies

An allergy happens when your body mistakes a harmless substance for a germ and overreacts to it. Food, plants, dust, pets, and many other substances can cause allergies.

Who gets allergies?

If you grow up in a large family or on a farm, your immune system will get lots of practice against germs. Some experts think this makes you less likely to get allergies.

Allergens

A substance that triggers an allergy is called an allergen.

 Wasp stings can kill people who are allergic to them.

 Antibiotic medicines can give allergic people a rash on the skin.

 Hair and **skin** from pets can cause an allergy very similar to hay fever.

 Molds grow in damp places. Their powdery spores can cause asthma.

 Some laundry detergents can cause a skin reaction.

Dust mites

Millions of these tiny beasts, which are smaller than periods, live in your home. They feed on dead skin. Their microscopic feces are a major cause of asthma.

Dust mites are related to spiders and have eight legs.

Mouth

What's the most common type of allergy?

Poison ivy

Skin allergies

If you touch a thing you're allergic to, itchy red spots may appear on your skin. Poison ivy plants, makeup, jewelry, and clothes can cause skin allergies.

Skin allergies cause itchy red spots that can look just like a nettle rash.

Food allergies

Foods that cause allergies include strawberries, nuts, seafood, and eggs. These can give an allergic person a skin rash, a runny nose, a sore mouth, nausea, and diarrhea.

Peanuts can be deadly to people with a nut allergy

Pollen

A very common cause of allergy is a powdery dust called pollen that is made by flowers. Pollen floats through the air and enters our bodies as we breathe.

Hay fever can make your eyes swollen, watery, and red.

Hay fever

People who are allergic to pollen have hay fever. When they breathe in lots of pollen, their noses run and their eyes get sore. Hay fever is worst in spring and summer, when grass flowers release lots of pollen into the air.

Inhalers squirt out medicine in a spray, helping people with asthma to breathe.

Asthma

People with asthma can find it hard to breathe. Their chests feel tight and their breathing becomes wheezy. Asthma can be caused by an allergy to dust mites, cat hair, or other substances in air.

Hay fever.

81

Digestive system

Food is made up of large, complicated chemicals that your body has to break into small chemicals that your blood can absorb. This process is called digestion.

Physical digestion
Some parts of your digestive system mash up food physically, just like a food processor does. Your mouth breaks food into chunks. Your stomach then churns these around until they form a slushy liquid.

Tube trip
Your digestive system is really just a long, tangled tube. Food travels about 30 feet (9 m) as it passes from start to finish.

When you swallow, food passes down a tube called the esophagus.

Become an expert...
on taste and smell, pages **36-37**
on what's in food, pages **106-107**

The Venus flytrap catches insects and digests them with enzymes.

Venus flytrap

Dragonfly

Chemical digestion
Many digestive organs make juices that break down the chemicals in food. The juices contain enzymes, which turn large food molecules into small molecules.

Liver

Large intestine

Small intestine

Rectum

Which is longer: your small intestine or your large intestine?

Digesting a meal

A large meal takes a day or more to pass through your digestive system. Different digestive organs make enzymes that work on different parts of the meal.

Bread starts to break down in your mouth.

Fat starts to break down in the small intestine.

The fiber in vegetables isn't digested.

Meat starts to break down in your stomach.

Stomach

6 pm
Food gets swallowed 10 seconds after it enters your mouth.

10 pm
A meal spends about 4 hours in the stomach, but very rich food can spend twice as long there.

3 am
The meal is slowly squeezed through your small intestine, sometimes causing loud gurgling noises.

The next day
Undigested leftovers reach the end of their journey about a day after you swallowed the food.

Curiosity quiz

Take a look through the digestive-system pages and see if you can spot any of the cells and tissues below.

Your small intestine.

Chew it over

We use our teeth to bite off and chew our food. During the course of your life, you will have two separate sets of teeth.

First teeth
Your first teeth start to grow when you're about 6 months old. The front teeth usually appear first.

Adult teeth
When you are six, your first teeth start to fall out. Adult teeth with deeper roots grow to replace them.

Wisdom teeth
Your back teeth are called wisdom teeth. They appear when you are 17 or older, and sometimes not at all.

False teeth
If you don't take care of your teeth, they will decay and fall out. Then you will need false teeth.

Types of teeth

Your mouth contains a selection of different types of teeth. Each type is designed to do a different job.

A child has 20 teeth; an adult has 32.

Molars at the back of your mouth have a flat edge so you can mash your food thoroughly.

Premolars roughly crush and grind your food. They are smaller than molars.

Canines grip and tear food using a single rounded point.

Incisors at the front of your mouth slice up chunks of food.

Roots

Without long roots, your teeth might break or fly out of your mouth if you bit down hard on your food. The root is held in place by a kind of cement.

What is another name for your first teeth?

Brush your teeth!

A sticky mixture of food and bacteria builds up on the surface of your teeth if you don't brush them properly. It is called plaque.

Brush twice a day to keep decay away.

Decay

Bacteria in plaque can eat through tooth enamel and attack the blood vessels and nerves deep inside the tooth. This is called decay. It hurts, and the dentist may need to give you a filling.

The sugar in candy sticks to your teeth, forming plaque. Plaque contains bacteria that causes teeth to decay.

Inside a tooth

Deep inside your teeth are lots of blood vessels and nerves. The nerves mean you can feel heat, cold, and pain.

Enamel

The hardest and toughest substance in your body is tooth enamel. It contains no living cells, so it can't repair itself if it is damaged.

Enamel

Blood vessels and nerves

Gum

Baby teeth or milk teeth.

From mouth to stomach

You start digesting food the moment you bite into it. As your teeth tear the food apart, enzymes in your spit begin to attack it chemically. By the time it reaches your stomach, your meal is unrecognizable.

Seen close up, your tongue is covered by tiny bumps and stalks that make its surface rough to improve its grip.

Get a grip

Your tongue is a super-strong, flexible bundle of muscle that pushes food against your teeth as you chew. It has a rough surface for good grip.

Mouth watering

The slimy liquid in your mouth is saliva. It moistens food to make it easier to chew and swallow. Saliva also contains an enzyme that breaks down starch, one of the main ingredients in bread, rice, and pasta.

Tongue   Uvula

What is the scientific name for burping?

This flap shuts off your nose when you swallow.

This flap closes your windpipe as you swallow.

Tongue

Swallowing

Swallowing is a reflex action, which means it happens automatically without your having to think about it. When your tongue pushes food to the back of the mouth, the swallowing reflex begins.

When your stomach is empty, its stretchy wall is full of folds.

Stretchy stomach

Your stomach has a very stretchy wall so that it can expand to hold big meals. Glands in the wall make acid and enzymes that start digesting protein in meat.

Down the tube

Swallowed food gets pushed down a muscular tube called the esophagus. The muscles work so well that you would still be able to swallow if you were standing on your head.

Food leaves your stomach through a small ring of muscle.

Stomach action

Your stomach's wall is made of muscles that squeeze in ripples to churn food around. When the food is ready to leave, the muscles squirt it out.

Inside the intestines

When food leaves your stomach, it enters a long, tangled tube. This has two parts. The first is your small intestine, which is long and narrow. The second is your large intestine, which is shorter but fatter.

Small intestine

The small intestine finishes off the job of digestion. Digested food soaks through its wall and enters the blood to be carried away.

Finger blobs
Tiny, finger-shaped blobs called villi line the small intestine. They speed up the absorption of food.

Muscles push food through your intestines just like this hand pushes a ball along a stocking.

A squeezing action travels along the intestine in waves.

Pushed along
Your intestines use a special kind of muscle action called peristalsis to move food along. Rings of muscle in the intestines squeeze behind the food, pushing it through.

How tall would you be if your intestines weren't coiled up?

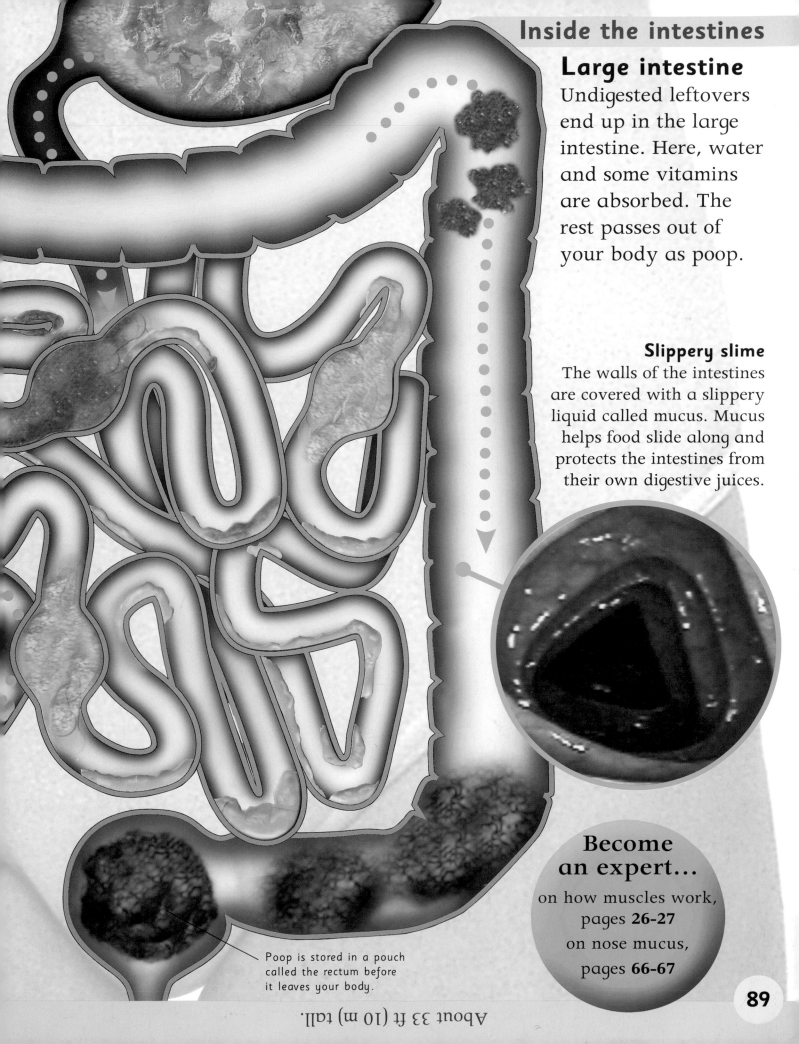

Large intestine

Undigested leftovers end up in the large intestine. Here, water and some vitamins are absorbed. The rest passes out of your body as poop.

Slippery slime

The walls of the intestines are covered with a slippery liquid called mucus. Mucus helps food slide along and protects the intestines from their own digestive juices.

Poop is stored in a pouch called the rectum before it leaves your body.

Become an expert...

on how muscles work, pages **26-27**

on nose mucus, pages **66-67**

About 33 ft (10 m) tall.

Waterworks

Your body gets rid of waste chemicals and excess water by making urine. Urine comes from two organs called kidneys. They filter and clean blood as it flows through, removing chemicals that your body doesn't need.

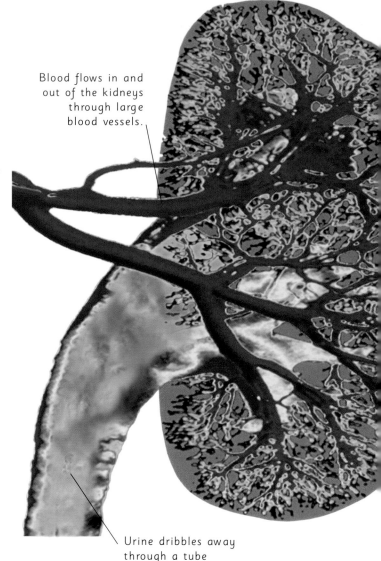

Blood flows in and out of the kidneys through large blood vessels.

Urine dribbles away through a tube called the ureter.

The kidneys clean your blood.

The ureters carry away urine.

The bladder stores urine.

The urethra gets rid of urine.

Urinary system

Your kidneys, bladder, and the tubes connected to them make up your urinary system. The last part of the urinary system is the urethra. Urine comes out of this tube when you go to the bathroom.

If you put your hands on your hips and your thumbs on your back, your kidneys are next to your thumb tips.

How long do your kidneys take to clean all the blood in your body?

Inside a kidney

The blood vessels entering your kidneys divide into smaller and smaller branches. These lead to a million tiny filtering units called nephrons.

Blood flows through a knot of tiny vessels.

Fluid passes out into a chamber.

The fluid leaves through this tube.

Inside a nephron

As blood flows through a nephron, fluids leave the blood vessel and pass to a long, looped tube. Useful chemicals are then reabsorbed into blood.

Water disposal

Here's how your body gets rid of water.

 Urine makes up more than half of the water that leaves your body.

 Breath contains over a quarter of the water your body gets rid of.

 Sweat is only about one-twelfth of the water leaving your body.

 Poop is fairly dry and contains only a little bit of your liquid waste.

Balancing act

Your kidneys keep the water level in your body perfectly balanced. If you drink too much, your kidneys make watery urine to get rid of any excess. When your body is short of water, your kidneys pass less into your urine.

This part of the brain monitors the water level in blood.

When the water level is low, the pituitary gland releases the hormone ADH.

A low water level also triggers a feeling of thirst, making you drink.

ADH travels to your kidneys in your blood.

Your kidneys save water, making your urine stronger.

Water control

Your kidneys work together with your brain to control your water level. When this level is low, your brain releases a hormone that makes your kidneys save water.

The stretchy bladder

All day long, a small stream of urine trickles out of each kidney. It collects in an organ called the bladder, which stores the urine until you go to the bathroom.

Diaper rash

Babies sometimes get a rash under their diapers. This happens when urine mixes with poop and makes the skin sore.

Filling up

Your bladder stretches as it fills up. This sends a signal to your brain, making you want to go to the bathroom.

X-ray of full bladder

X-ray of empty bladder

Full stretch

An adult's bladder stretches from the size of a plum to the size of a grapefruit and can hold about 1 pint (500 ml) of urine. Your bladder is about the size of an orange when it's full.

The bladder's muscly wall squeezes to push urine out.

Grapefruit   Orange   Plum

Inside the bladder

The bladder has a waterproof lining to stop it from leaking. Urine leaves through a tube called the urethra, which is normally held shut by two muscles.

How much urine do you make each day?

What is urine?

Urine is made of water and waste chemicals. The main waste is urea, which your body makes when it breaks down protein. The color of urine depends on how much you drink. If you drink lots of water, your urine will turn pale.

The yellow color comes from a chemical that is made when old blood cells are broken down.

Tubes called ureters bring urine from the kidneys.

This muscle opens automatically when the bladder is full.

Urethra

We have to learn to control this muscle.

Camel urine

Camels can last for months without water so they can survive in the driest deserts. They save water by making thick, syrupy urine that is twice as salty as seawater.

Camels store fat in their humps, which they use for energy.

Bladder control

In young children, the muscles that open the bladder work automatically. As children get older, they learn to control one of the muscles.

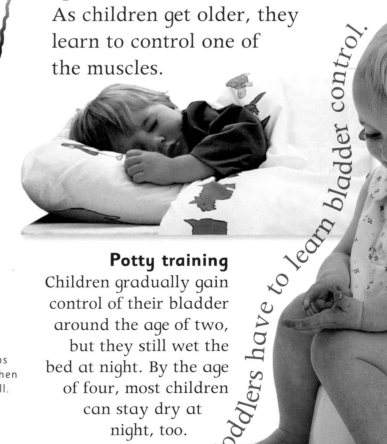

Toddlers have to learn bladder control.

Potty training

Children gradually gain control of their bladder around the age of two, but they still wet the bed at night. By the age of four, most children can stay dry at night, too.

4–8 cups, depending on how much you drink and sweat.

Making a baby

You need a mother and a father to make a baby. The mother's body does most of the work, but the father also has an important job—his sperm joins with the mother's egg, and a new life begins...

The first cells
After 36 hours, the cell has divided and made an exact copy of itself. These are the first two cells of a baby.

Eggs are the biggest cells in the human body. But they are still very small—ten would fit across a pinhead.

Sperm are amazing viewed under a microscope. They look like tiny tadpoles. You can see their tails wriggling as they swim.

Sperm race
Millions of sperm swim toward the egg cell. Only one sperm can join with the egg to make a new cell.

By the time the baby is born, the fertilized cell will have become 100 trillion cells.

94

Divide again
You don't grow much in the first few days. The two cells divide to make four, then eight, and so on.

The future you
Each cell is unique to you. Cells are full of instructions about what you will look like.

At three days
The cells have kept on dividing. There are now 16 cells, and they are almost ready to plant themselves in the uterus.

Where it all happens
The sperm fertilizes the egg in a tunnel, called a fallopian tube. The fertilized egg moves down the tunnel toward the mother's uterus. The journey takes about five days.

The cells start dividing as they move down the fallopian tube toward the uterus.

Millions of sperm from the father travel up here toward the egg.

This is the mother's ovary. It releases one egg every month.

This is the uterus. It is about the size of a pear and has muscular walls.

Arriving in the uterus
The ball of cells plants itself in the wall of the uterus. In this warm, dark place, the baby will spend the next 40 weeks growing and developing.

Growing in the womb

By eight weeks old, the baby is no longer a bundle of cells. It looks like a tiny person and is called a fetus. The fetus does not eat, drink, or breathe by itself. All its needs are taken care of by its mother.

Boy or girl?

Parents can find out about a baby's health and sex before it is born. A scanning machine shows the baby on a screen. This is many parents' first sight of their child.

Parents often choose not to find out their child's sex so they will be surprised on the day it is born.

Eight weeks old.

The size of a strawberry
The fetus has eyes, a nose, lips, and a tongue. It lives in a protective bag of liquid and uses its tiny muscles to swim around gracefully.

Sixteen weeks old.

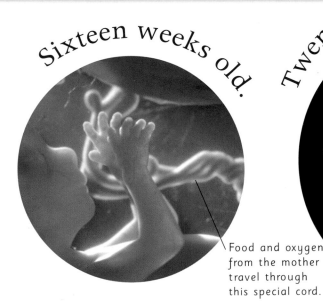

Food and oxygen from the mother travel through this special cord.

The size of a lemon
At 16 weeks, the fetus can make different faces, clench its fist, and suck its thumb. It can hear its first sounds, but its eyes are not open yet.

Twenty weeks old.

The size of a grapefruit
At 20 weeks, the fetus is getting more active. It is still quite small, so there's plenty of room to kick around and do somersaults.

When do we first start to dream?

Twenty-two weeks old.

You might feel the baby move if you put your hand on a pregnant woman's tummy.

Fuzzy fetus

By 22 weeks, the baby is quite well developed but fairly thin. It will spend the next few weeks growing a layer of fat under its skin. It is covered in soft, fine hair.

What's it like in there?

It is quite noisy in the womb with the sounds of the mother's heartbeat and stomach rumbles. The baby can also hear noises outside the womb, and loud bangs may make it jump. It learns to recognize its mother's voice long before it is born.

Happy birthday!

At last, after around 40 weeks, the moment comes for the baby to be born. Newborn babies can breathe, suck, and swallow. They communicate by crying if they are hungry or feel uncomfortable.

Identical twins

Identical twins are made when a fertilized egg splits into two separate cell clusters.

Fertilization occurs when a single sperm fuses with the egg.

The fertilized egg splits into two. We don't know what makes this happen.

Two cell clusters develop into two separate babies.

Nonidentical twins

Nonidentical twins are made when the mother releases two eggs instead of one.

Each egg is fertilized by a different sperm. Two babies then develop.

Growing up

Identical twins often notice amazing similarities in their tastes and behavior. Sometimes they can even tell what the other is thinking!

Double trouble

There are two different types of twins—identical and nonidentical. Identical twins have the same genes. Nonidentical twins are like any other brother or sister, so only half their genes are the same.

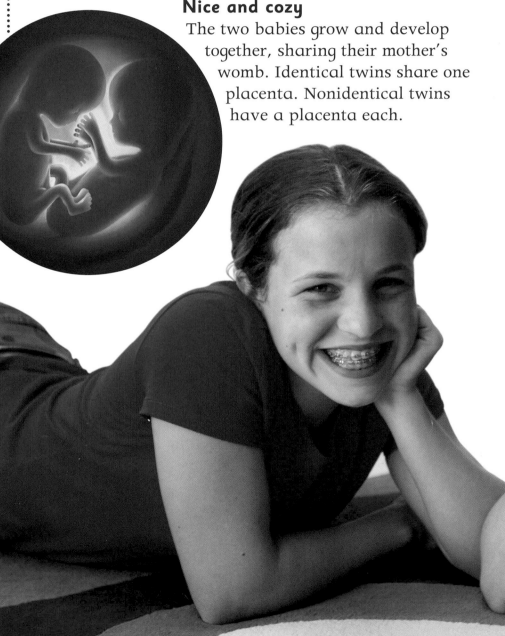

Nice and cozy
The two babies grow and develop together, sharing their mother's womb. Identical twins share one placenta. Nonidentical twins have a placenta each.

Do identical twins have exactly the same fingerprints?

Multiple births

Even rarer than being a twin is being a triplet, or even a quadruplet...

 Triplets: One in 8,100 natural pregnancies produces triplets.

 Quadruplets: It's rarer to be a quad. One in 729,000 pregnancies produces quads.

 Quintuplets: Having five children is usually a result of fertility treatment.

 Sextuplets: There are currently only around 30 sets of six in the world.

Twins in the family

Once a couple has had one set of twins, they are more likely to have another. Also, if your mother, or *her* mother, is a nonidentical twin, you may inherit the trait and have twins yourself!

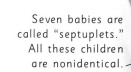

Mirror twins

Some identical twins are called mirror twins. Often, one will be left-handed and the other right-handed, and their fingerprints appear to mirror each other.

Seven babies are called "septuplets." All these children are nonidentical.

Record-breakers!

There are presently only two sets of septuplets in the world. These are named Kenneth, Brandon, Nathan, Joel, Alexis, Natalie, and Kelsey. They were born in Iowa in 1997.

No, because the soft skin on their fingertips was molded differently in the womb.

The early years

Babies' bodies grow very fast, but their brains develop quickly, too. Learning to move around and talk are both huge tasks.

Big head

Babies have enormous heads in relation to the size of their bodies! As you get older, the rest of your body catches up.

Babies' big heads hold big brains! They need them because there's lots to learn.

New skills

Children's brains are changing all the time as they learn new skills at an amazing rate.

 Smiling: most babies start to smile at around 6 weeks old.

 Drinking: babies learn to drink from a lidded cup between 6 and 12 months.

 Eating: most babies can feed themselves from a bowl at around 15 months.

 Learning colors: children can name colors by 3 years old.

 Brushing teeth: 5 year olds can brush their teeth without help.

Your body grows very fast during your first year...

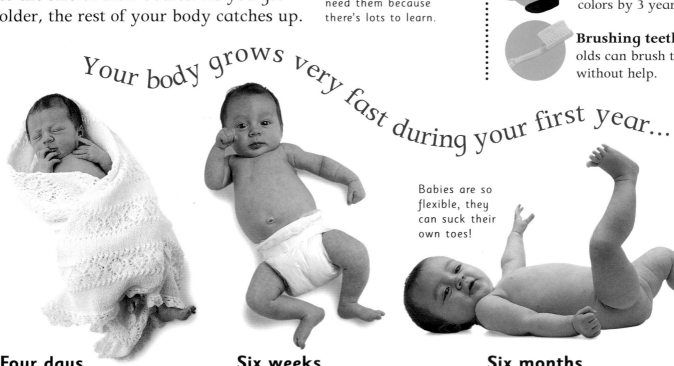

Babies are so flexible, they can suck their own toes!

Four days

Newborns spend most of their time asleep. Even when they're awake, they don't open their eyes much.

Six weeks

Babies cry when they are cold or hungry. By this age, they start to make cooing sounds, too.

Six months

Babies have a lot more control over their bodies now. Their muscles are stronger, so they can sit up without help.

When do you reach half your adult height?

Being able to talk makes it easier to play with other children.

Chatterbox

By one year, a baby is trying to speak. By two, children can use 100 different words, and by three most know more than 1000 different words.

...and hardly slows down during your second!

By three, children know the difference between boys and girls.

Two years

Children this age can walk and run, climb stairs, and kick balls. They are starting to get dressed alone but can't fasten buttons, zippers, buckles, and shoelaces.

One year

By this age, babies can understand simple words. They also take their first few steps.

101

Life cycle

Growing up

As a child, you learn to walk and talk, run and jump, go to the bathroom alone, eat with cutlery, read and write, and make friends!

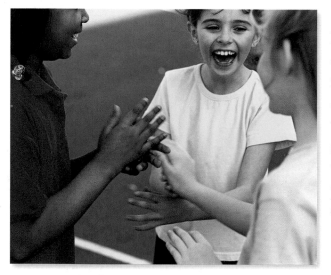

Making friends

By five years old, children can form friendships and play together. They start to care what other people think of them.

What can you do?

Do you realize how much work goes into learning all these amazing skills?

 Shoelaces: At six years old, most children can tie their own shoelaces.

 Riding a bike: At seven, many children can ride a two-wheeled bike.

 Reading: Some children learn to read at four, some at five, and some at six!

 Writing: You should write fairly clearly by the time you are seven.

As your baby fat melts away, your features become clearer...

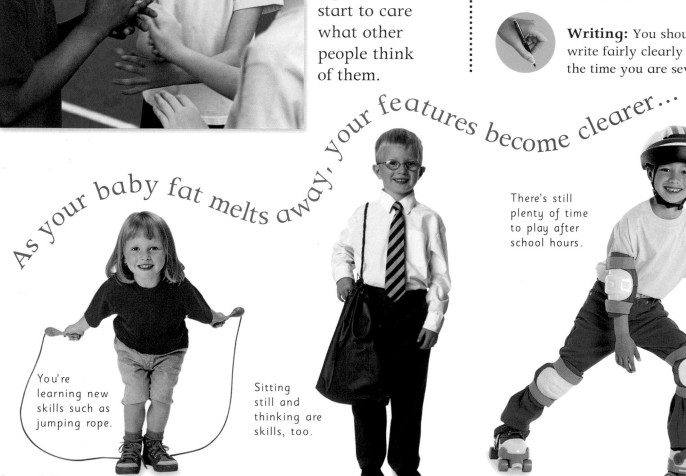

You're learning new skills such as jumping rope.

Sitting still and thinking are skills, too.

There's still plenty of time to play after school hours.

Age 4-5
By this age, a child can speak clearly in basic sentences, and knows many thousands of words.

Age 5-6
It's time to learn to read, write, add and subtract, and maybe even start playing a musical instrument.

Age 7-10
Boys and girls often like different things at this age, so they have more friends of their own sex.

102

What makes you grow?

Hair is here!

During puberty, both boys and girls get more hair on their bodies. Boys also start to grow hair on their faces and may start to shave.

...and you look more like you!

Times when you grow fast are called growth spurts.

During adolescence, your thoughts and feelings change as much as your body.

Age 11-13

Your body is about to start growing very fast again. Boys have their growth spurt a year or two later than girls.

What's next?

The time when you are more than a child but not quite grown up is called adolescence. Your body changes a huge amount, which is known as puberty.

103

Growth hormone, a chemical produced by your pituitary gland.

Growing older

Adults keep growing, but more slowly than children. When you get older, your body takes longer to repair itself and replace worn-out cells.

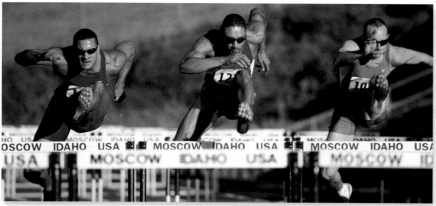

Twenties
During your twenties, you are at your peak. Your body has reached its adult size so you don't spend most of your energy on growing.

Brittle bones
With old age, the bones and disks in the spine get weaker and thinner, so people get a little bit shorter.

A normal, healthy spine holds the body straight.

The spine starts to weaken.

Eventually, it forms an "s" curve and the head moves forward.

Life expectancy
As a general rule, the bigger a creature is, the longer it lives. So how long do humans live?

 Butterflies have very short lives. Many live for only a month or two.

 Cats kept indoors as pets live longer than wild ones—usually about 15 years.

 People can live for 100 years. Women generally live longer than men.

 Tortoises can live for 150 years. Some spend a quarter of their lives asleep.

Thirties
Because they're not growing any more, many people need to eat less so they don't get fat. Most bodies are strong and healthy, but athletes are already past their best.

What is the longest a person has ever lived?

Smile lines

With age, skin gets less stretchy and will not smooth out when you relax your face. This is gives you wrinkles. Many cultures respect wrinkles as signs of wisdom and experience.

Silver surfer

Today, people live longer than ever, thanks to advances in medicine. A healthy diet, exercise, and a young mind can make old age a happy time.

Old age

Papery skin, weak bones, stiff joints, and bad eyesight are common in old people. Most of the organs, including the lungs and heart, don't work as well as they used to.

As you get older, your hair contains less melanin—the substance that gives it its color.

Middle age

Organs and muscles are starting to get weaker. Skin on the face gets wrinkly, and hair starts to turn gray. Women stop having babies.

Records prove that a French woman, Jeanne-Louise Calment, lived for 122 years.

What's in food?

People eat to get energy. You need a variety of foods to keep your body in peak working condition.

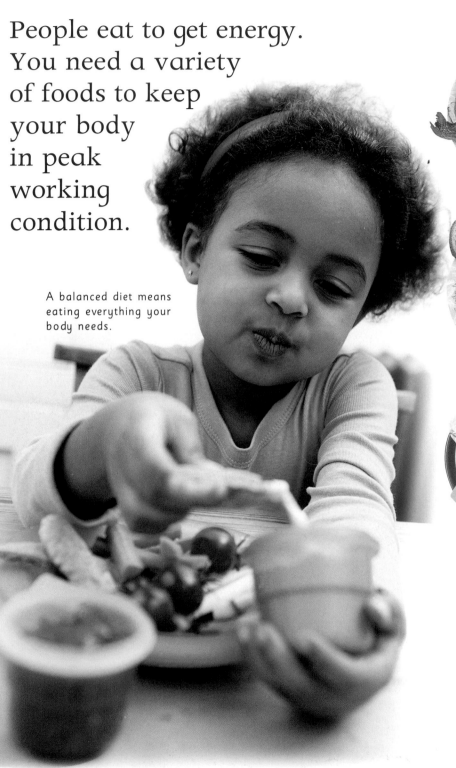

A balanced diet means eating everything your body needs.

Proteins
Meat, fish, eggs, beans, and nuts contain protein. Your body needs protein to repair its cells.

Carbohydrates
Bread, cereal, pasta, and sweet foods are mostly carbohydrates. You need them to give you energy.

Fat
Nuts and dairy foods, such as butter and cheese, contain fat. You only need small amounts of fat.

Fast food and cola are nice as a treat, but they're no substitute for a good meal.

Eat your greens
Fresh fruits and vegetables are crammed with vitamins and minerals. Your body needs these to stay healthy.

Junk food
Fast foods like hamburgers and chips contain unhealthy amounts of fat and salt, and few vitamins.

What is a vegetarian?

Water

Your body is two-thirds water, but you're losing water all the time. You could live for several weeks without food, but only for about 3 days without water.

You need about six glasses of liquid every day, but some of this can come from your food.

Allergies

If your body reacts badly to a certain food and makes you sick, you may be allergic to it.

Wheat isn't good for some people. They cannot eat normal bread.

Nuts can be dangerous—even in tiny quantities—if you have a nut allergy.

Cows' milk doesn't suit some people, but they can drink sheep or goats' milk.

Sunshine food

You need vitamin D for strong bones. It is found in fish and eggs, but your body can produce it when you get sunlight on your skin.

Food gives you energy.

Become an expert...

on chewing food, pages **86-87**
on making urine, pages **90-91**

Fuel for your body

An orange gives you enough energy to cycle for 5 minutes. A chocolate bar gives you enough energy to cycle for 45 minutes.

The amount of energy you get from food is measured in calories.

A person who does not eat meat.

Sleep

When you sleep, your body rests. Your brain stops dealing with things in the outside world, and uses this time to sort out the events of the day.

Adults need about seven hours of sleep.

A newborn baby can sleep for 20 hours a day. By six months, 15 hours is usually enough.

A three-year-old needs about 12 hours of sleep.

How much sleep?

As we grow older, we need less sleep. Young adults need about eight hours, while people over 60 may need only six.

Sleep patterns

Throughout the night, you move in and out of shallow and deep sleep several times. As the hours pass, sleep gradually becomes lighter until you wake up.

Time for bed.

Awake

Shallow sleep

The yellow dots show

Deep sleep

9   10   11   12   1

What is insomnia?

Dreaming

Everyone dreams. When you dream, your eyelids flicker. This is called rapid eye movement, or REM, sleep.

Nightmares

Nightmares are scary dreams that can wake you up and make you feel frightened or sad. During nightmares, people often think they are being chased or bullied.

When you dream, anything is ...possible!

Everyone dreams, but not everyone remembers their dreams.

What dreams mean

People are fascinated by what dreams mean. We don't know for sure, but...

Flying can mean that you feel powerful and free of problems.

Being naked sometimes means you are afraid of being weak.

Falling may mean you feel out of control or are scared of losing something.

Sleepwalking

During deep sleep, parts of the brain stay awake. People may talk, or get up and walk around. They usually don't remember that they have done this.

when you dream

2 3 4 5 6

Good morning!

The medical name for being unable to fall or stay asleep.

Doctors and dentists

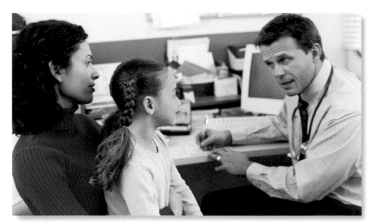

When you are sick, you visit the doctor. First, the doctor examines you. Next, the doctor prescribes treatment or medicine to make you better.

The examination

The doctor asks you about your symptoms and then looks at and listens to different parts of your body.

Say "ah"

The doctor uses a stick to hold your tongue down and look at your tonsils. If your tonsils often get infected, you may need an operation to remove them.

Ears, nose, and throat

Doctors use an otoscope to examine your ears, nose, and throat. Swelling or itchiness may mean you have an infection.

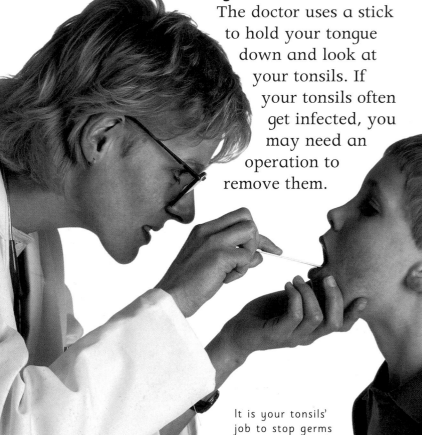

It is your tonsils' job to stop germs from getting down your throat.

Hear, hear

Doctors use an instrument called a stethoscope to listen to your heartbeat or to hear how well your lungs are working.

110

What is a pediatrician?

Tools of the trade

Doctors keep a few simple instruments in their offices to help them examine their patients.

A stethoscope allows the doctor to listen to your heart or your breathing.

A rubber hammer is tapped against your knee to test your reflexes.

An ophthalmoscope has a bright light for looking at the back of your eyes.

Syringes are used to give people injections to stop them getting some diseases.

Medicine comes from a pharmacy. The doctor just gives you a prescription.

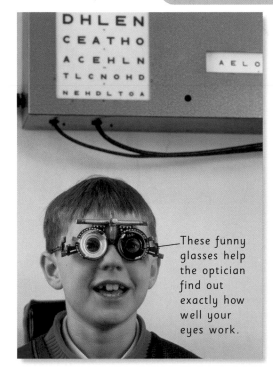

These funny glasses help the optician find out exactly how well your eyes work.

Eye spy

Opticians test your sight to find out whether you need glasses. They test each eye separately because often one can see better than the other. Your eyesight changes, so you need to get your eyes tested every year.

Open wide

You can care for your teeth by brushing them, but you should still get them checked twice a year by a dentist. Hopefully, you won't need any fillings.

Brace yourself
Orthodontists are dentists who straighten out crooked teeth. They do this by fitting your mouth with braces to push your teeth gradually into the right position.

A doctor who specializes in children's illnesses.

Body language

You don't just talk with words—you also use your hands, face, and body. The look on your face and the way you stand can say a lot about how you really feel.

Personal space

People show how well they know each other by how close they stand or how often they touch. It's rude to stand too close to a stranger but normal to stand close to a best friend.

Only best friends and family can enter the **close intimate zone**.

The **intimate zone** is where people who know you well can stand while talking to you.

The **personal zone** is for people who know you but aren't close, such as teachers.

The **social zone** is where strangers stand while talking to you.

These girls are copying each other's body language.

Copying

Good friends often mimic each other's body language without realizing it. They might walk in step, sit or stand in the same position, or copy each other's hand movements.

Who's in charge?

One of the things people signal with their body is whether they're in charge or somebody else is in charge. Leaning forward or looking relaxed are ways of appearing to be in charge.

This boy's relaxed posture shows he feels very confident.

How does a dog show it knows you're in charge?

Learning gestures

You pick up a lot of your body language from the people you grow up with. Your gestures and the way you sit, stand, and walk are probably similar to those of your friends and family.

Boys often learn their gestures from older brothers, and girls pick up many of theirs from older sisters.

Open or closed?

When someone feels relaxed or friendly, they have an "open" posture, with arms and legs apart. If someone is nervous or awkward, they have a "closed" posture, with arms and legs close to the body.

Talking to animals

Animals can't understand speech, but they often understand our body language. Dogs can sense who's in charge from body language. They need to be treated kindly but firmly or they will start to misbehave.

Become an expert...

on muscles and movement, pages **26–27**

Use your hands

Most people move their hands as they speak, but what do their gestures mean? Some hand gestures mean the same thing all over the world, but others vary from place to place.

Talk to the hands

Hands seem to have minds of their own. When people talk, their hands move all over the place, even when they're on the phone!

Thumbs up
A raised thumb means "good" or "well done!" in North America. In Germany it means "one," in Japan it means "five," and in the Middle East and Africa it's a rude gesture.

Making a circle
A finger touching a thumb means "OK" in North America, "worthless" in France, and "I want my change in coins" in Japan. In Turkey it can be rude.

Palms together
This is a sign of prayer in Christian countries, but in India it is used as a greeting. Indians place their hands together, make a slight bow, and say *Namaste*.

Shaking hands
Shaking hands is a common greeting in many countries, but there are slight differences. A firm handshake is a sign of sincerity in Europe but is thought to be aggressive in Asia.

In some countries, women never shake hands with men.

In Sicily, this gesture combined with a karate chopping movement means "I hate you so much."

How does a diver say "shark" underwater?

Pointing with an outstretched arm means something is far away.

Making a point
Pointing is one of the first hand gestures that people learn, and it means the same thing all over the world. Babies ask for things by pointing at them before they learn to speak.

Become an expert...
on the bones in your hands, page **20-21**

These 26 signs stand for the letters of the alphabet in British sign language.

Two fingers on the palm means the letter "n."

Talking underwater
Divers can't speak underwater, so they use a kind of sign language instead. They have special signs for marine animals like sharks and turtles.

OK is shown by a finger touching a thumb, making a circle.

Stay at this depth is shown by waving a flat hand from side to side.

Stop is shown by a clenched fist and a bent arm.

Sign language
Deaf people communicate without hearing by reading lips, using facial expressions, or using sign language. Sign language varies a lot from country to country.

By making a shark's fin on the head with one hand.

Express yourself

Your face helps you communicate by showing how you feel. All over the world, people use the same facial expressions to show the six main emotions.

Surprise makes you gasp for breath because the hormone adrenaline makes your lungs work faster.

2 Surprised
When you're surprised, your eyebrows shoot up, your eyes open wide, and your jaw drops. Some people clap the side of their face or cover their mouth as well.

1 Happy
In a genuine smile, the eyes crease and the cheeks rise. A smile means the same thing whether you live in the Sahara Desert or the Amazon rainforest.

Crabby or angry people sometimes look red around the eyes.

3 Angry
An angry person's eyebrows move down, their eyes narrow, and their mouth closes tightly. They might also glare without blinking.

How many facial expression are there?

Baby face

Babies communicate with their faces before they learn to talk. They smile, frown, and show all the main emotions.

Babies learn to mirror their parents' smiles from a very early age.

Become an expert...

on how babies develop, pages **100-101**

5 Afraid
Fear raises the eyelids, making the eyes look white. The mouth opens wide in horror, and blood may drain from the face, making the skin pale.

4 Sad
In an unhappy face, the mouth droops, the inner ends of the eyebrows go up, and wrinkles appear above the nose. Powerful feelings of sadness also make people cry.

6 Disgusted
Wrinkles across the nose and narrow eyes are signs of disgust. The sight of disgust in someone's face can make you feel disgusted, too.

About 7,000.

Amazing facts about YOU!

Skeleton and bones

Without a skeleton to hold you up, you'd collapse on the ground like a pile of jelly.

 Your smallest bone is the stapes in your ear, which is smaller than a rice grain.

 Weight for weight, bones are stronger than steel or concrete.

 A baby has more than 300 bones, but adults have only 206.

Muscles and movement

Muscles move your body by pulling bones. You use hundreds of them when you walk.

Every hair in your body has a tiny muscle that can pull it upright.

Your strongest muscle is the masseter (jaw muscle), which closes your mouth.

You use more muscles when you frown than when you smile.

Brain and nerves

Your brain is the body's control center. Signals zoom to and from the brain along your nerves.

 Nerves carry signals at up to 250 mph (400 km/h).

 Your brain is made of about 100 billion tiny cells called neurons.

 The left side of your brain controls the right side of your body and vice versa.

 The human eye can see a candle flame at night from 1 mile (1.6 km) away.

 When you're bored, the pupils in your eyes get smaller.

Heart and blood

Your heart pumps blood around your body. It works nonstop without getting tired.

 Your smallest blood vessels are ten times thinner than a hair.

 Your body contains enough blood vessels to circle the world twice.

Breathing

Lungs take air into your body so that life-giving oxygen can enter your blood.

 Laid out, the inside of your lungs would be a third as big as a tennis court.

 The fastest recorded sneeze reached 104 mph (167 km/h).

 In one day, you breathe in enough air to fill 33,000 soda cans.

Skin, nails and hair

The tough, protective surface of your body is almost entirely dead.

 Every four years, you shed your own body weight in dead skin.

 You have about 5 million hairs, but only 100,000 are on your head.

The thickest skin on your body is on the soles of your feet.

Fighting disease

Germs are always trying to get inside you, but your body fights back.

Lassa fever is a very dangerous disease. It kills about a fifth of its victims.

Bacteria are so small that a thousand could fit on the head of a pin.

The world's most common disease is the common cold.

Cancer happens when your own cells multiply out of control.

When you recover from an infectious disease, your body becomes immune to it.

Digestive system

Digestion turns food into simple chemicals that your body can make into new cells or use for fuel.

The food you eat in a year weighs as much as a car.

You make enough spit in your lifetime to fill two swimming pools.

Your digestive glands start working as soon as you smell or see food.

Your tongue senses five tastes: salty, sweet, sour, bitter, and savory.

The smell of poop comes from a chemical called skatole.

Each hair on your head grows for about 3 or 4 years and then falls out. A new one grows in its place.

Urinary system

Urine gets rid of chemicals that your body doesn't need.

You will make enough urine in your lifetime to fill 500 bathtubs.

Asparagus can turn your urine green. Blackberries can turn it red.

Reproduction

The reproductive organs create new people from tiny specks of matter.

The most babies born to one mother is 69. Most were twins, triplets, or quads.

The first quintuplets known to have survived infancy were born in 1934.

Growth

As you grow, you slowly change into an adult, but it takes a long time!

The fastest-growing part of a baby's body is its head.

A girl is about three-quarters of her adult height at 7 years old.

A boy is about three-quarters of his adult height at 9 years old.

Through the ages

The human body is so amazingly complicated that it's taken doctors at least 4,000 years to figure out how it works. Their discoveries have led to many new ways of curing illness.

460–377 BC

The Greek doctor Hippocrates is sometimes called the father of medicine. He was one of the first people to realize that diseases have natural causes and cures.

Before the time of Hippocrates, many people thought that diseases were punishments sent by the gods.

250 BC Egyptian doctors cut open corpses to find out how the body works.

100 BC Chinese doctors discover that blood travels around the body in cycles.

1290 Spectacles are worn for the first time in Venice, Italy.

1350 Rats spread bubonic plague in Europe, killing a quarter of the people.

1500 A Swiss pig farmer performs the first cesarian section on a living person.

1596 Italian scientist Galileo Galilei invents the thermometer.

1684 Dutch microscopist Anton van Leeuwenhoek discovers blood cells.

1770 The world's first comfortable false teeth are used in France.

1796 English surgeon Edward Jenner discovers how to make vaccines.

1816 The stethoscope is used for the first time.

What life-saving antibiotic did Alexander Fleming discover?

Italian scientist Lazzaro Spallanzani ate his own vomit over and over to find out how the stomach works.

 1818 James Blundell carries out the first blood transfusion.

 1852 Doctors use bandages soaked in plaster to make casts.

 1853 Scottish doctor Alexander Wood invents the syringe.

 1895 Wilhelm Röntgen accidentally discovers how to take X-rays of bones.

 1928 An English scientist discovers antibiotics—drugs that kill bacteria.

 1953 Scientists work out the structure of DNA, the chemical that carries genes.

 1955 Doctors start using ultrasound scanners to see babies inside the womb.

 1967 Surgeon Christiaan Barnard carries out the first heart transplant.

 1971 Brain scanners come into use, allowing doctors to study living brains.

 1978 Louise Joy Brown, the first test-tube baby, is born in England.

Modern medicine

Doctors know more about how the body works than ever before, but there are still some mysteries, like why we hiccup or how the brain works.

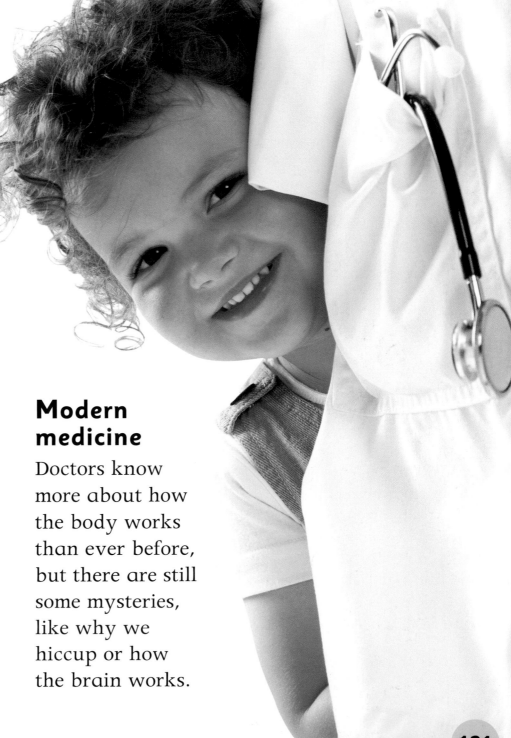

Penicillin.

Glossary

Artery A blood vessel that carries blood away from your heart to the rest of your body.

Bacteria Tiny one-celled creatures found all around us. Some are helpful, others cause diseases.

Blood vessel Any tube that carries blood through your body.

Capillary The smallest type of blood vessel. Your body contains thousands of miles of capillaries.

Cell The smallest living unit of your body.

Diaphragm A strong, flat sheet of muscle under your lungs. You use it when you breathe.

Digestion The process that breaks down food into tiny pieces that your body can absorb and use.

Enzyme A substance that speeds up a particular chemical reaction in the body. Digestive enzymes speed up the breakdown of food molecules.

Epiglottis A "trap door" of skin that stops food from going into your breathing tubes when you swallow.

Esophagus The tube from your mouth that takes food to your stomach when you swallow.

Genes Instructions that control the way your body develops and works. Genes pass from parents to their children.

Germs Tiny living things that can get into your body and cause illness. Bacteria and viruses are germs.

Gland A group of specialized cells that make and release a particular substance, such as a hormone or enzyme.

Hormone A chemical produced by one part of the body in order to change the way a different part of the body works. Hormones are made in glands and carried by the blood.

Joint A connection between two bones.

Mucus Slippery liquid on the inside of your nose, throat, and intestines.

Nerves Threads of tissue that carry high-speed signals around the body.

Nutrients The basic chemicals that make up food. Your body uses nutrients for fuel, growth, and repair.

Organ A group of tissues that form a body part designed for a specific job. Your stomach is an organ.

Oxygen One of the gases in the air. You need to breathe in oxygen to live.

Proteins Vital nutrients that help your body build new cells. Food such as meat, eggs, fish, and cheese are rich in proteins.

Receptor A type of nerve cell that detects a change outside or inside the body, helping to create one of the senses. Touch receptors in the skin, for example, help create the sense of touch.

Reflex A reaction that is out of your control, like breathing or blinking when something gets near your eyes.

Saliva The liquid in your mouth. Saliva helps you taste, swallow, and digest food.

System A group of organs that work together. Your mouth, stomach, and intestines make up your digestive system.

Tissue A group of cells that look and act the same. Muscle is a type of tissue.

Umbilical cord The tube joining a baby to its mother's body while it is still inside her.

Urine Waste liquid that passes out of you when you go to the bathroom. Urine is made of water and chemicals your body doesn't need.

Vaccination A substance that is swallowed or injected to protect your body from disease.

Vein A blood vessel that carries blood toward your heart.

Vertebra One of the bones that link together to form your backbone, or spine.

X-rays Invisible rays that pass through objects. X-ray photographs show the inside of your body.

Index

Reference section

Picture credits

The publisher would like to thank the following for their kind permission to reproduce their images:

(Key: a-above; c-center; b-below; l-left; r-right; t-top)

4 Corbis: Larry Williams (c); Science Photo Library: (bc); Getty Images: Barbara Peacock (cl). 5 Alamy Images: Aflo Foto Agency (tc), Janine Wiedel Photolibrary (cra), Pictor (cr); Corbis: Reuters (cla); Science Photo Library: (tr), Dr. Gopal Murti (crb), VVG (br). 6 Corbis: Laura Doss. 7 Alamy Images: Goodshoot (tr), Janine Wiedel Photolibrary (tc); Corbis: Jose Luis Pelaez (bl); 8 Science Photo Library: Dr. Gopal Murti (br), Martin Dohrn (cra). 9 Science Photo Library: (jar 3); Andrew Syred (tr), Prof. Aaron Polliack (jar 2), VVG (cl), (jar 1), (jar 4). 10 Alamy Images: RubberBall Productions (r); Corbis: Thom Lang (cl brain) Science Photo Library: J.L. Martra, Publiphoto Diffusion (bl); Victor de Schwanberg (cl heart), (cl kidney). 11 Alamy Images: Ablestock (bl), Comstock Images (button 5); Pictor (t), RubberBall Productions (c), (button 2). 13 DK Images: Oxford University Museum (ca); Science Photo Library: Pascal Goetgheluck (bl). 14 Science Photo Library: Sovereign ISM (bl). 15 Science Photo Library: D. Roberts (bl), Michael Donne, University of Manchester (br). 18 Science Photo Library: Andrew Syred (br), CNRI (cr), VVG (bl). 19 Alamy Images: Medical-on-line (cla); Science Photo Library: (cr), Department of Clinical Radiology, Salisbury District Hospital (tc), VVG (crb). 20 Alamy Images: Superstock (b); Science Photo Library: VVG (cr). 20-21 Science Photo Library: (t). 23 Science Photo Library: Mehua Kulyk (cl); Getty Images: David Roth (crb). 24 Science Photo Library: Astrid & Hans-Frieder Michler (cla), Prof. P. Motta/Dept. of Anatomy/University "La Sapienza" (bl), Victor de Schwanberg (clb), VVG (cl). 25 Corbis: Kevin R. Morris (r). 26 Corbis: (l). 27 Corbis: Tom & Dee Ann McCarthy (clb). 28 Corbis: Ed Bock (tr), Thierry Orban/Sygma (cl); 28-29 Getty Images: Mike Timo. 29 Science Photo Library: Keith, Custom Medical Stock Photo (tl). 30 Getty Images: BodyOnline (c). 31 Corbis: Bryan F. Peterson (crb), Warren Morgan (bl); Colour Vision Store: (crbb); Science Photo Library: Dr. Goran Bredberg (crb), Mehau Kulyk (cra), Nancy Kedersha (tr), Omikron (cr). 32 Corbis: Jim Craigmyle (tl); Science Photo Library: Nancy Kedersha (br). 33 Corbis: Christine Osborne (tr); Science Photo Library: Michael Donne (tl). 34-35 Corbis: Norbert Schaefer (c), 35 Science Photo Library: Joe Bator (cb). 36 ImageState/Pictor: StockImage (cl); Science Photo Library: Omikron (br). 37 Science Photo Library: CNRI (br); Getty Images: Ross Whitaker (tl). 38 Science Photo Library: Gusto (bl). 40 Corbis: Lee White (background). 41 Alamy Images: BananaStock (br); 41 Corbis: Lee White (ca), (c); Colour Vision Store: (tr); 41 Science Photo Library: David Becker (cl). 42 DK Images: Natural History Museum (button 5); Science Photo Library: Mehau Kulyk (l). 44 Getty Images: Ross Whitaker (br). 46 Corbis: Tom Stewart (r). 47

Corbis: Dave G. Houser (tr), Firefly Productions (cb); Science Photo Library: Dr. Goran Bredberg (bc). 49 Science Photo Library: Susumu Nishinaga (tc). 51 Science Photo Library: CNRI (crb), Dr. P. Marazzi (br), NIBSC (cra), (cr). 52 Science Photo Library: Susumu Nishinaga (br), VVG (cr). 53 Science Photo Library: NIBSC (cl). 54 Science Photo Library: BSPI, Gilles (bl), Professors P.M. Motta & S. Correr (tl); Roger Harris (cb). 54-55 Science Photo Library: Dr. Yogas Nikas (b). 55 Science Photo Library: (tl), NIBSC (tr), Roger Harris (c). 56 Corbis: Tom Stewart (bl); Science Photo Library: CNRI (cr). 57 Alamy Images: Shout (button 1); Photolibrary.com: Leanne Temme (cl); Science Photo Library: Alex Bartel (button 4), Astrid & Hanns-Frieder Michler (button 3), Martin Dohrn (tl). 58 Getty Images: Erin Patrice O'Brien (b). 63 Corbis: Stephen Frink (cr); Science Photo Library: David M. Martin M.D. (cla), Mark Thomas (tl), Matt Meadows, Peter Arnold Inc. (br), Proff. Motta, Correr & Nottola/University "La Sapienza", Rome (crb). 64 Science Photo Library: Hank Morgan (cra). 65 Bubbles: Ian West (cl); Corbis: Don Mason (tl), Paul A. Souders (br); Getty Images: Stephanie Rausser (ca). 66 Science Photo Library: Damien Lovegrove (l), Matt Meadows, Peter Arnold Inc. (tr), Proff. Motta, Correr & Nottola/University "La Sapienza", Rome (cr). 68 Alamy Images: Phoebe Dunn (cra); Science Photo Library: Andrew Syred (crb), (br); VVG (c). 69 Alamy Images: Pixland (tl). ImageState/Pictor: (bl). 70 Science Photo Library: VVG (bc). 71 Science Photo Library: Andrew Syred (ca); Lauren Shear (bc); Getty Images: Daniel J. Cox (tr). 72 Science Photo Library: VVG (ca). 73 Science Photo Library: Alex Bartel (tr), Martin Dohrn (c), VVG (br), (background). 74 DK Images: AMNH (tr blue), (tr green); Science Photo Library: Dr. Jeremy Burgess (br); Getty Images: Suzanne ann Nick Geary (bl). 75 DK Images: AMNH (button 1); Photolibrary.com: OSF (tr); Science Photo Library: Dr. Kari Lounatamaa (cla), Eye of Science (br), John Hadfield (cb). 76 Science Photo Library: Biophoto Associates (cl), Custom Medical Stock Photo (tc), Prof P.Motta/Dept of Anatomy/University, "La Sapienza", Rome (br). 77 Science Photo Library: CNRI (bc), Professoers P.M. Motta, K.R. Porter & P.M. Andrews (ca). 78 DK Images: AMNH (tr); Science Photo Library: Biology Media (br). 79 Science Photo Library: BSIP Estiot (tr); Getty Images: Chris Harvey (cl), Steven Peters (tl). 80 Corbis: Paul A. Souders (cl); Science Photo Library: Andrew Syred (button 4), Dr. Jeremy Burgess (button 1), K.H. Kjeldsen (b). 81 Corbis: Lester V. Bergman (cla); Getty Image: Digital Vision (br); Science Photo Library: Dr. Jeremy Burgess (tr), Dr. P. Marazzi (cr), Mark Clarke (bc). 83 Science Photo Library: BSIP, Cavallini James (crb), David

M. Martin M.D. (br) Gusto Productions (cra), VVG (cr). 84 Corbis: Michael Keller (car); Powerstock: age fotostock (tl); Science Photo Library: Gusto Productions (tr). 85 Science Photo Library: Hattie Young (tl). 86 Science Photo Library: Dr. P. Marazzi (bl), Tek Image (tl), VVG (c). 87 Science Photo Library: David. M. Martin M.D. (c); Zefa Visual Media: Chad Johnston/Masterfile (l). 88 Science Photo Library: David M. Martin M.D. (c) Eye of Science (cl). 89 Science Photo Library: David M. Martin M.D. (cr). 92 Science Photo Library: (c), (cr), BSIP, Cavallini James (tr). 93 Alamy Images: Robert Harding (tr). 94 Robert Harding Picture Library: (c). Science Photo Library: Christian Darkin (tr). 95 Science Photo Library: Dr. Yorgos Nikas (tl), (tc), (tr). 96 Penny Arlon (ca); Mother & Baby Picture Library: Ian Hooton (tr); Photolibrary.com: OSF (br); Science Photo Library: Dr. G. Moscoso (bl), Edelmann (bc). 97 Alamy Images: BM2 (tl); Photolibrary.com: OSF (tr); Getty Images: Ross Whitaker (bc). 98 Getty Images: (c). 98-99 Alamy Images: Big Cheese Photo (b). 99 Alamy Images: Robert Llewellyn (tr), Brooks Kraft (br). 101 Corbis: Strauss/Curtis (tl). 102 Corbis: O'Brien Productions (cl). 103 Corbis: Larry Williams (r); Rex Features: Phanie Agency/PHN (tl). 104 Corbis: Pete Saloutos cl. 104-105 Science Photo Library: Alfred Pasieka bl; Blustone (b). 105 Corbis: Roy Morsch (tr); Getty Images: Yann Layma (tl). 107 Corbis: Norbert Schaefer (tr); Zefa Visual Media: Robert Karpa/Masterfile (tc). 110 ImageState/Pictor: (tl), (cr). 111 Science Photo Library: Adam Hart-Davis (tc), Michael Donne (br), Pascal Goetgheluck (clb). 113 Corbis: Ariel Skelley (cl); Getty Images: Erin Patrice O'Brien (r). 114 Getty Images: Ian Sanderson (tr). 117 Corbis: Mark Tuschman (c); Getty Images: Tim Flach (tl). 118 Science Photo Library: Astrid & Hanns-Frieder Michler (button 1). 119 DK Images: Judith Miller/Elms Letsers (button 1); Science Photo Library: Dr. Tony Brain (button 2). 120 DK Images: British Museum (button 1), Judith Miller/TW conroy (button 9). 121 Corbis: Larry Williams (button 4), Michael Pole (r); Science Photo Library: (button 4), Edelmann (button 7), Victor de Schwanberg (button 8). 125 Alamy Images: RubberBall Productions. 126-127 Alamy Images: Aflo Foto Agency

All other images © Dorling Kindersley
www.dkimages.com

Acknowledgments

Dorling Kindersley would like to thank: Elinor Greenwood, Lorrie Mack, and Fleur Star for editorial assistance, Dorian Spencer Davies for additional illustration, Mary Sandberg for additional design assistance, Julia Harris-Voss for picture research, and Chris Bernstein for compiling the index.

The end

J 612 Fir

Human body encyclopedia

for the United States
of America.

do ordain and establish
this Constitution

to ourselves
and our Posterity,

and secure the
Blessings of Liberty

promote the
general Welfare,

provide for the
common defense,

insure domestic Tranquility,

establish Justice,

in order to form
a more perfect Union,

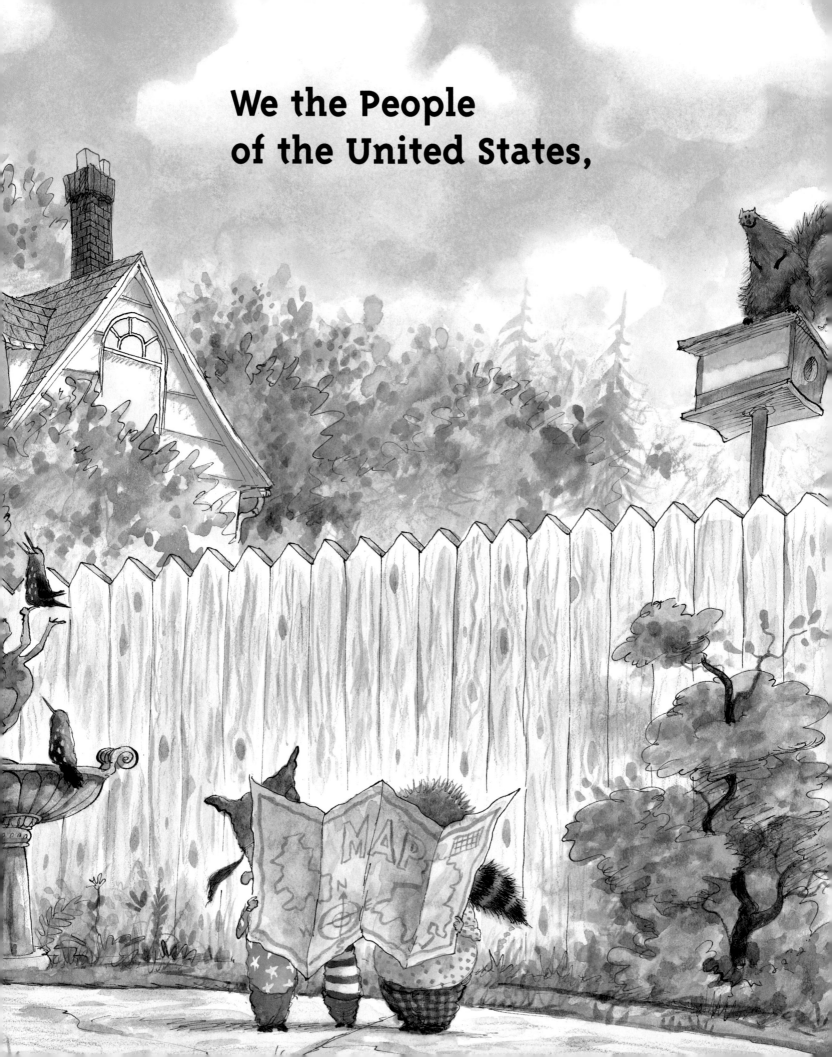

We the People
of the United States,

The Words in the Preamble and What They Mean . . .

PREAMBLE: The first part of something, an introduction.

WE THE PEOPLE OF THE UNITED STATES: All the people in our country, including kids.

IN ORDER TO FORM A MORE PERFECT UNION: To come together and make things better for everyone who lives in our country.

ESTABLISH JUSTICE: To make things fair and honest for everyone.

INSURE DOMESTIC TRANQUILITY: To make sure we can all have a nice life and get along with one another.

PROVIDE FOR THE COMMON DEFENSE: To protect us from other people or countries who might try to harm us, as in a war, and to help us if we have been harmed.

PROMOTE THE GENERAL WELFARE: To help make life good for everybody. Having enough to eat, a place to live, being safe, and having friends and fun times are some of the things that make our lives good.

AND SECURE THE BLESSINGS OF LIBERTY: To protect our rights and freedoms and not let anyone take them away. Being able to choose our religion, to say what we think, and to get together with friends, family, and other people are some of the freedoms we have.

TO OURSELVES AND OUR POSTERITY: For kids, parents, other grown-ups, and all the people born in our country after we are.

DO ORDAIN AND ESTABLISH THIS CONSTITUTION: To write down, and then to live by, a list of rules and promises for our government to keep and our people to obey.

FOR THE UNITED STATES OF AMERICA: Our country—where we live.

These big words expressed big ideas.
Check out what the dog is doing in this story.
He will also help you understand what they mean.

A few years ago I went and saw the real Constitution in Washington, D.C. It's an old, brown, crackly-looking thing with curly handwriting that's almost impossible to read. But when it was new, it gave us rights and privileges that nobody had ever had before. It let us decide for ourselves what kind of life we wanted to have. At certain times I wanted to be a garbage man, baseball player, brain surgeon, and airline pilot. Instead I became a dad, an artist, and a political cartoonist. When I paint my paintings or draw my cartoons, I can do them any way I want. Being able to do that makes me feel very happy and very free. And I think that's exactly what all those old guys with their big words and big ideas wanted—for themselves, for me, for other grown-ups, and, maybe especially, for kids.

BIG WORDS, BIG IDEAS

The first time I was forced to think about the Constitution was in fifth grade. Presidents' Day was coming up and my teacher, Mrs. Baldwin, wanted to talk about BIG IDEAS!: stuff like FREEDOM, LIBERTY, FOUNDING FATHERS, PRESIDENTS. I sat doodling a picture of George Washington riding the red 27" Johnnie Ginger Mountain Ranger bike I hoped to get for my next birthday.

"WE THE PEOPLE OF THE UNITED STATES, IN ORDER TO FORM A MORE PERFECT UNION . . ." she recited, "SECURE THE BLESSINGS OF LIBERTY TO OURSELVES AND OUR POSTERITY . . ."

I remember thinking: MAN, why couldn't the guys who wrote this just use regular English?

"ESTABLISH JUSTICE, INSURE DOMESTIC TRANQUILITY . . ." But I guess that's just how everyone talked back in the olden times— like my grandfather, who always said things like "ripsnortin'," "hornswoggled," and "rooty-tooty."

I'm a much older guy now and I've figured out that our Constitution is simply a list of rules and promises written down by people just like you and me. Some were tall, some were short, some were thin, fat, or hairy, and all of them used to be kids. So you definitely don't have to be a grown-up to understand what they wrote.

For me, the Constitution is a kind of how-to book, showing us ways to have happiness, safety, and comfort. Sounds like common sense, right? But a couple hundred years ago those things weren't common AT ALL. For instance, back then if you said or wrote something and the people in charge didn't like it, they could put you in jail or stick tar and feathers all over you (ouch!). Now, even though a lot has changed, if you listen, the rules in our Constitution still make good sense— and tar is used to make highways and feathers are strictly for the birds.

For Deborah

Published by Dial Books for Young Readers
A division of Penguin Putnam Inc.
345 Hudson Street
New York, New York 10014
Illustrations and foreword copyright © 2002 by David Catrow
All rights reserved
Designed by Lily Malcom
Text set in Triplex Serif Bold
Printed in Hong Kong on acid-free paper
10 9 8 7 6 5 4 3 2 1
Catrow, David.
We the kids : the preamble to the Constitution of the United States /
illustrations and foreword by David Catrow.
p. cm.
Summary: A humorously illustrated preamble to
the Constitution of the United States.
ISBN 0-8037-2553-1
1. Constitutional law—United States—Juvenile literature.
[1. Constitutional law—United States.]   I. Title.
KF4550.Z9 C38 2002
342.73'02—dc21
2001042350

The art was created using pencil and watercolor.

We the Kids

The Preamble to
the Constitution of the United States

illustrations and foreword by
David Catrow

Dial Books for Young Readers
New York